Money for Life

Everyone's Guide to Financial Freedom

Alvin Hall
with Alex Prud'homme

CORONET BOOKS
Hodder & Stoughton

Copyright © 2000 Alvin Hall

The right of Alvin Hall to be identified as the Author
of the Work has been asserted by him in accordance with
the Copyright, Designs and Patents Act 1988.

First published in Great Britain in 2000
by Hodder and Stoughton
First published in this revised edition in 2000
by Hodder and Stoughton
A division of Hodder Headline

A Coronet Paperback

10 9 8 7

British Library Cataloguing in Publication Data

Hall, Alvin D.
Money for life: everyone's guide to financial freedom
1. Finance, Personal
I. Title
332′.024

ISBN 0 340 79321 X

Typeset by Hewer Text Ltd, Edinburgh
Printed and bound in Great Britain by
Clays Ltd, St Ives plc

Hodder and Stoughton
A division of Hodder Headline
338 Euston Road
London NW1 3BH

MONEY FOR LIFE

This book is dedicated to the memory of my grandmother, Rosa Lee Hall, whose simple wisdoms I carry with me every day

ACKNOWLEDGEMENTS

Robert McKenzie, who commissioned the first series of *Your Money or Your Life* from TalkBack Productions and served as associate producer of the second series and producer of the third series, deserves special thanks for his generosity and frank criticism as he read and reread the manuscript of this book. Other people whose skills and knowledge were useful in helping to keep this book 'on the money' are Nigel Johnson-Hill, David McMasters (Killik and Co.), Jason Ball (Integrated Investments) and Maya Weil.

Karl Weber, my agent and friend, not only brought Alex Prud'homme and me together to write this book, he also helped us to give shape to the material, contributed his exceptional editorial skills and supported us all the way – working with us until we mailed the final copy of the manuscript. Cat Ledger, who represented this project in the UK, played an important and helpful role. Alex Prud'homme could not have been a more ideal writing companion. He deserves lots of praise for digesting a wealth of complicated material and then skilfully translating my classroom and television conversational style to the written page.

The *Your Money or Your Life* team's research, perseverance and creativity must be praised. Richard Farmbrough, the series editor, was exceptionally supportive and forthright. He used these qualities to get the best work and information out of me and repaid my work by creating an informative and entertaining show. Beatrice Gay and Belinda Gregg, the production managers, always made me feel cared for and Ali Cardy, the production runner, made the long filming days enjoyable by her thoughtful attention to my little quirks. Thanks to the directors, especially Marielle Weise (for playing my lucky song), and to cameraman Steve Weiser and sound recordist, Glenn Bates, for their patience, honesty and compulsive attention to detail. Even my mother said I never looked or sounded better.

At various times in my life, I've been lucky enough to meet people who have taken a chance on me, opened doors and given me an opportunity to grow. Thanks to Daisy Goodwin, the series editor, who auditioned me for the series and selected me as presenter for *Your Money or Your Life*. Thanks also to Rowena Webb at Hodder and Stoughton for writing the letter asking me whether I would be interested in writing this book. And finally, none of this would have been possible without Jonathan Drori, the guy I met in the Photographer's Gallery in Leicester Square, who originally selected me to present my first BBC series, *Alvin Hall's Guide to Successful Investing*. Words cannot express my gratitude for Jonathan's ongoing belief in me – and for his guidance and friendship.

Alvin Hall
New York, New York
October 2000

CONTENTS

INTRODUCTION

'You don't have to make the same mistakes as other people in order to learn the right lessons. You just need to watch and listen.'

This is one of the earliest, and most valuable, pieces of advice that my grandmother, Rosa Lee Hall, passed on to me. Little did I imagine that this kernel of wisdom, slipped into conversation as we were fishing in my small, rural hometown of Wakulla, Florida, would become the guiding principle of a book I would write about money years later.

Money for Life grew out of my own experience – the fears, misperceptions, mistakes and self-delusions that I had about money, as well as my gradual understanding of how money works, the interest I took in the people and mechanisms of the marketplace and the growing confidence I had in my own ability to build wealth and to explain it.

Illustrated with stories (all of which have been altered) from my life and the lives of people I've known, this book aims to clear away some of the myths about the 'mystery' of money, and offers common-sense tips on how to save, invest and spend wisely. In these stories, you may recognise your own aspirations for – or struggles with – budgeting and the accumulation of wealth. Among other things, I have laid out practical steps for:

- controlling your spending impulses
- eliminating debt
- building your nest-egg
- finding financial help
- minding the cost of a relationship
- getting a mortgage
- planning for your retirement

And I have provided an overview of important financial products, such as stocks, bonds and unit trusts. But this is not a text book, and I encourage you to use it as you like – read it straight through, or skip around from section to section. *Money for Life* will help you to deal with the money in *your* life.

Don't expect New Age lingo or get-rich-quick tips from this book – I'm still too much of a pragmatic country boy for that. I will attempt to explain the sometimes daunting subject of money in a straightforward, entertaining way. In fact, much of what you'll see in these pages should seem quite sensible to you – as if you already know this material, or could have figured it out for yourself, or you heard it from a friend.

In taping *Your Money or Your Life,* my BBC television series about personal finance, I've heard many permutations of the same dreams and excuses people have about money. Usually, people like to talk about:

- 'What I'd do if I had a lot of money.'
- 'How come I don't have a lot of money?'
- 'Why I can't handle money.'

It seems to be a common belief that if you suddenly come into a lot of money – perhaps by winning the lottery – the clouds will part, a ray of sunshine will strike you on the forehead and the ancient wisdoms of money management will suddenly be revealed. Well, to paraphrase Bette Davis in *What Ever Happened to Baby Jane?*: 'It ain't gonna happen, Blanche!'

The only way to learn about money is to educate yourself, think about what you are doing and learn through trial and error.

It isn't easy, I know. As we set out in life, many of us are ignorant of how money works, or are scared of it, and so we avoid thinking too much about it. This, of course, is how we begin to get ourselves into trouble. With time, we hopefully learn a few lessons, stop making mistakes and are better able to take care of ourselves. At least, that's the idea. But the truth is that we often repeat our old bad habits – to a lesser degree, or in new ways – again and again. In fact, too many of us don't bother to take the time to reflect on our experiences and glean the financial lessons embedded within them. And because of a general reluctance to talk about money, even within the family, the lessons are easily lost or are never understood in the first place.

This is why my grandmother's advice is so important. If we keep our eyes and ears open, and pay attention, we can all learn new things. I was mystified by money for years. But when I made it a priority to learn how it works, I was surprised at how quickly I began to understand it; and once the subject had been demystified, I really began to enjoy it. When all is said and done, money is not terribly difficult to understand and is not something to be scared of.

I still make mistakes myself, of course – but I try to make fewer and less dramatic errors than some of the financial fiascoes I will tell you about here. The point is that sometimes it is in facing our weaknesses head-on that we make the greatest strides in self-improvement. This is as true in financial matters as it is in the rest of life. My aim is to pass on what I've learned through trial and error, in the hope that it will save you time, energy and, of course, money.

Perhaps you've had your own problems with money, or want to know more about the subject, or have a specific financial agenda. If so, you might recognise yourself in one of the following anecdotes from my life:

- If you feel overwhelmed by the idea of money, and don't even want to talk about it – then you are like I was as a young man.

Raised poor and black in the wealthiest country in the world, I had always been surrounded by mixed messages about money. For a long time it seemed like a great and distant 'other' – a force so vast and incomprehensible that it meant almost nothing to me. Yet, in America there is an obsessive cult around wealth. 'Money is the grease that makes life slide,' people say. 'There are only two reasons to get married – money, and more money.' 'Money can't buy happiness, but it *can* buy a first-class ticket as you search for it.' These are all the kinds of phrases that added to the mystique of money.

To make things even more confusing, I attended an élite New England college, where one simply didn't talk about money – it was considered vulgar – and for a while I adopted that reticent attitude (not that I had any money to talk about). But when I found myself trapped in debt and a dead-end job, I had a 'Eureka!' moment: I realised that it was essential for me to talk about money, and to understand how it worked, so that I could change my life. Now, of course, I talk about money all the time; indeed, I make a living explaining how it works.

- If you're budget-challenged – the type of person who says, 'I don't worry about money, I just spend it' – then you and my twenty-something self have a lot in common.

Have you ever charged all of your credit cards to the limit, tried to fool yourself by throwing your bills into the bin, and/or gone through a period of living for the moment without a budget or a clue? Well, I've been there, done that and bought the T-shirt – on my maxed-out credit card! As a friend of mine said: 'Your salary was gone before you could spend it.'

I think of this phase as my 'financial adolescence' (complete with growing pains), and not surprisingly it was a difficult period. By day I was a mild-mannered English teacher, making a paltry wage; by night, armed with a pocket full of credit cards, I turned into a Spending Monster who bought everything from designer clothing to fancy kitchen utensils. While the Baptist core within me never believed that I *deserved* these luxury goods, the Spending Monster said I should have everything I wanted because I could *almost* afford them. I didn't understand how credit card debt works, and I got myself into a lot of trouble.

Indeed, many people get caught in this trap, and don't *want* to leave: the cycle of overspending, debt accumulation and denial repeats and repeats, self-destructively.

Although I have reformed, and am quite financially disciplined now, I continue to struggle with my weaknesses. Indeed, I am half-afraid that my inner Spending Monster will one day jump out of my body like the creature in the *Alien* movies, steal my Platinum card and go on a berserk buying spree on Savile Row.

- If you are simply curious about money, you are the kind of person I became after I began to earn a decent salary, saved it and invested it according to a well-thought-out plan.

My financial education began in the late 1970s when I decided to change my career and learn how money works. In the meantime, some of my college friends and acquaintances had become very well-to-do in what seemed a miraculously short period. For me, deliverance came from a friend who offered me a job at his father's Wall Street training firm. Seeing this as an opportunity, I committed myself totally to learning about the financial markets – and I discovered, much to my surprise, that I actually enjoyed them. I became fascinated by how a person's ideas grew, branching like a tree, into real money.

Three specific questions intrigued me: how do people accumulate money? How do they hold on to it and make it work for them? And if there is a secret to money, why couldn't I figure it out?

During this time my rent was eating up 60 per cent of my take-home pay, and my diet was dictated by whatever was on special offer. I knew all of the sale cycles at my favourite stores, and rarely paid full price: my rule was 30 per cent off, or I'd walk out the door! The fiscal discipline was good for me, and I enjoyed the challenge.

As my salary grew, I did not allow myself to revert to my old shop-'til-you-drop habits. I limited my use of credit cards, and began to put money away for holidays, better clothing (always) and for rainy days.

Despite my affection for money, I have never been interested in accumulating tons and tons of the stuff. Indeed, the longer I studied finance, the more deeply fascinated I became with the intellectual side of the markets – they are reminiscent of complex, whirring mechanisms, replete with gears, chambers and trap doors (not to mention smoke and mirrors). Today, I continue to be more absorbed with the ideas that explain how people build wealth, and the means by which they do so, than in building my own gold-plated Temple of Dendur.

- If you are determined to build up enough money to insulate yourself from life's nasty surprises, and to treat yourself once in a while, then you are like I was when I lost my job security.

    Those rainy days we save up for always arrive unexpectedly, and I was shocked the day my friend's Wall

Street training company was sold. While I did not lose my job right then, I realised that no company could guarantee me a lifelong safety net. I knew I'd have to become totally responsible for myself and my financial future. And the very next day I began to take action – with a determination that surprised even me. In that moment, something about my relationship and attitude towards money had changed for ever.

I remember going through the process of creating a financial plan for myself, repeating, 'You've got to keep it simple, stupid!', over and over again. I wanted to make my plan as fail-safe as possible.

I had seen friends with elaborate ideas about how they were going to make a killing get slaughtered by the market. I had watched people who bet on virtually anything, and rarely won. And I had heard stories of people who piled up debt in pursuit of not-well-thought-through ideas falling short. On the other hand, I had also seen people – some of them former students of mine on Wall Street – who had started with little capital but a lot of determination, achieve their goals. As my grandmother had advised, I watched and listened, and used other people's experiences as signposts to guide me to ways to save money, buy a flat and invest part of my income. It worked, and I, too, was able to achieve my goals.

Years later, when I was made redundant at a job that I really liked, I was able to cope with it emotionally because I had prepared myself financially. After my last day on that job, I took a taxi straight to Tiffany's. For years, I had wanted a set of scalloped-shaped celadon bowls made by Raynaud & Company. Previously, I hadn't let myself buy them because they were just too expensive. That day, however, I bought four of them: if I was going to be out of work, I decided, then I wanted to eat cereal out of bowls that I loved!

Extravagant? Foolish? Perhaps. But by this time I knew myself well enough to understand that an occasional indulgence is essential to keep myself going. The secret, as always with treats, is knowing where to draw the line.

It's strange: money is one of the most important factors in our lives, and yet it is one of the few things that many people are willing to abdicate all responsibility for – whether to their parents, a spouse, a partner, a financial adviser, or, most commonly, to the winds of Fate.

Which of the following phrases have you heard yourself say?

- 'I hate maths, and I don't *do* budgets or bills.'
- 'The State will take care of me.'
- 'I wish I had someone to do this for me.'

I hear these excuses constantly – and if memory serves I've even used a few of them myself over the years. But the fact is, *you* are responsible for how you earn your money, how you use your money and how you make your money work for you. This does not require you to kow-tow to a golden statue of Gordon Gekko, or make a blood pact with Mammon. It is simply about learning to be responsible for yourself and those people who are dependent on you. Don't procrastinate. Do take action. Stay the course for the long term. And keep your eyes and ears open. I hope the stories and ideas in this book will enable you to understand that achieving your financial goals can be easier and more satisfying than you may imagine.

At the end of the day, I would be pleased if you took from this book a few common-sense lessons that will help you effect real, positive change in your life – whether it's buying a house, building up your savings, expanding your investment horizons, or even communicating in a better way about finance with your loved ones. Indeed, with a little planning, action, diligence and luck you *will* have more money for your life.

CHAPTER 1

IN A NEW YORK MINUTE:
A CHEAT-SHEET
FOR READERS IN A HURRY

The Alvin Hall Quick Quiz on Personal Finance

- Have you ever tracked all of your expenses for a month? Does the thought of doing so frighten you?
- Do you have enough money saved to support yourself for at least three months if you should lose your income?
- Do you pay your credit card debt in full, on time, every month? If not, do you know how much you owe?
- Do you make and stick to a budget while you're on holiday?
- Do you contribute to a pension?
- Do you know the level of life assurance you should have, and have you bought an appropriate policy?
- Do you have a will?

If you answered 'Yes' to five or more of these questions, then you probably have the foundations for healthy financial habits. If you answered 'No' to three or more, then you may be heading for the budget blues – quickly.

I f you're the kind of reader who peeks ahead to the last page of a whodunit – or if you haven't the time or patience to read the whole of this book right now – this chapter offers an overview of the topics I will discuss later. It gets to the heart of the matter in a New York minute, and gives you the most important steps towards establishing a firm financial footing.

On the other hand, we New Yorkers tend to do everything too fast for our own good. If you really want to learn the key points of wealth building and how to avoid the debt trap – not to mention the story of my twenty-nine credit cards; the unusual place my grandmother stashed her savings; and the 'Alvin Hall Law of Sex' – then I strongly encourage you to read all of the following chapters.

As a whole, this book aims to provide a common-sense guide to helping you understand and gain control of your personal financial life. Whether you read it straight through, or skip around and read the chapters that interest you most, you'll see that money is not that hard to understand and that your goals are within reach.

The seven fundamental points listed below will give you a good start towards developing healthy financial habits.

KNOW YOUR FINANCIAL SELF

The interconnectedness of money and our emotions is often stronger than we are aware of or want to admit. Indeed, money can summon stronger feelings to the surface than almost any subject other than love. Some people use money as a shield, which protects them from the world, or as a pair of wings, which allows them to soar; lack of money has the opposite effect, of course, and summons up feelings of sinking vulnerability.

Because these emotions are so difficult to talk about, it is hard to view money from a dispassionate distance. But many people could benefit from doing so. Try to take an honest look at your strengths, weaknesses, biases and assumptions about money. Only when you have a clear understanding of your spending and saving habits – what I call your 'money personality' – can you begin to manage your finances properly.

One way to do this is to track your spending for a week or month. It's a useful – and sometimes shocking – exercise in self-revelation.

A few years ago, for example, I became worried that although I was earning a very nice salary on Wall Street I wasn't able to hold on to most of it. Where was all of my money going, I wondered. Like a scientist on the trail of a new disease – in this case my own spending virus – I undertook an experiment: I bought a diary and wrote down every purchase I made over the course of one month. It was tedious, but what I discovered at the end was that I was spending consistently on food and housing, and recklessly on clothing and items on 'sale'.

I am well known as a clothes-horse, but I didn't realise quite how much money I was spending on my habit every month. Examining my diary, I saw that I had been buying impulsively; I had allowed my emotions rather than my intellect to rule my wallet. On further reflection, I realised that I had been using money as a shield. As a boy, I was very thin and as an adult I wanted to appear more substantial; nice, new clothes allowed me to remake myself in that image. As I stared at myself in the financial mirror, I realised that although I was beautifully outfitted, I needed to change my spending habits. I had thirty-five suits at the time, many of which I did not wear very often, so I gave half of them away; now I allow only twelve suits in my closet. Further, I hold myself back from buying clothes on impulse. Today, when I see a beautiful suit or coat, I wait at least fortyeight hours before buying it, just to make sure I really need *that* coat at *that* price at *that* particular time. Like a person in the first blush of lust, I sometimes need a cool-down period; the fortyeight-hour wait is like a cold shower on my shopping passions. Usually I come to my senses and discover that the item I thought I *needed* was really only something I *wanted*, and I don't buy it.

We tend to be the most reckless when we use money as I did, as a shield, or as a way to soar. You can't control everything about yourself, but if you try to guard against that kind of emotional spending, you will greatly increase the likelihood of achieving the personal and financial success that you desire.

PAY YOURSELF FIRST: SAVE MORE, SPEND LESS

Saving should be your *top* priority. After you've covered essential monthly expenses – such as food, rent and utilities – you should put money away before you spend it on things you want rather than need.

The essence of this lesson is to 'pay yourself first'. That is, get in the habit of putting a fixed amount of your income into savings and/or investments every month before you decide to spend on something new. The purpose of this is to ensure that your money is going towards things that are really important, such as the long-term happiness of you and your family, before you spend it on non-essentials such as a fancy new car, a night on the town, or a piece of clothing that will just hang in the wardrobe.

While this piece of advice might sound simple enough, many people find it hard to accomplish with any consistency. Teaching an old dog new tricks is never easy – especially when you are both the dog and the trainer – but teaching yourself to put money away every month is a worthwhile trick to master.

The key is to make saving a regular habit. Set yourself a goal, and try to save a certain amount of money each week or month, even if it's only a small amount. Don't worry too much at first about how much you save, or where you save it; just learn to make it a habit. Once you start saving on a regular basis, you'll be amazed at how quickly your nest-egg grows.

We all face a constant battle of wills between the Angel of Saving and the Devil of Spending. Sometimes you need a trick to give the Angel the upper hand. What I do is deduct 10 per cent of every payment I receive – whether it's a pay cheque or just the repayment of a loan to a friend – and put it into my savings. At first this was a real struggle and I was inconsistent. But with time I learned the trick and now I try to save an even higher percentage of my income. The Angel of Saving would say I am rewarding myself with this habit; just as quickly, however, the Devil of Spending reminds me that I now have more money to spend – but I've grown deaf in that ear.

Another way to develop the saving habit – especially if you are freelance or an independent consultant – is to think of yourself as a small business: every month you receive income (your pay cheque) and have expenses (family, mortgage, credit cards, student loan, etc.).

As the head of your company, you are the only generator of income – the company's primary asset – and your main priority is to invest in the future of your company. The best way to do this is to pay yourself first by making deposits into your savings account or making other appropriate investments.

Your first objective is to build a cushion for emergencies. Your goal should be to save at least three to six months' worth of living expenses. I know that's a lot of money . . . it certainly was for me when I set this goal for myself. Having acheived it, I'm now even more conservative (or paranoid) than that: I am freelance and if I somehow lost my work, my recovery time would be longer than for someone employed by a large company. What if my car refused to start, or I lost the use of a major appliance such as a cooker or refrigerator? To guard against such financial pitfalls, I keep a full year's worth of living expenses in a risk-free savings account. While I may not be earning much interest on this money, it allows me to sleep well at night.

Use the money in your current account to pay your daily living expenses, and keep the money in your savings account off-limits. And bear in mind the power of compounding, by which you earn interest on your interest (see page 80).

Once you've saved enough for emergencies, you can then look at saving elsewhere. You should aim to contribute to tax-free investments, such as National Savings Certificates, or a cash ISA (Individual Savings Account), a government-sponsored tax-free savings scheme.

Whatever you do, don't spend more than you earn, and don't save your hard-earned money in the cookie jar: the only interest that money will attract is from the mice . . . or a burglar!

DEBT IS A FOUR-LETTER WORD

Being in debt today is not like being in debt two hundred years ago: back then, if you didn't repay your lenders on time you could end up in one of Britain's debtors' prisons, like the one on London's Clink Street – squalid places filled with all sorts of human specimens, even the odd delinquent priest, many of whom were left to literally rot away in chains. Today, lenders are less likely to stick you in thumbscrews than to hand you one credit card after another, while encouraging you to spend more, more, *more*, as quickly as possible.

Indeed, Britons today owe a staggering £13 billion on their plastic. How can this be? Well, the short answer is that the card issuers are making money from lending you all of that.

Think of credit cards like a box of rich, dark chocolate: if someone sends you a box, you will be tempted to eat every single one of those delicious morsels; and your debt, like your waist-line, will keep expanding. But don't blame the credit card companies: look in the mirror. Debt is *your* problem and only *you* can solve it.

Now don't get me wrong, I like credit cards – they are one of the simplest and best ways of spending money without laying out cash – but the catch (and there is always a catch) is that you must pay your bills in full and on time, every month. If you don't, and especially if you make only the minimum monthly payment, then every time you use the card, interest starts to accumulate on your debt *immediately*, which makes paying off your loan more costly and time-consuming.

Credit card debt is one of the most common ways that people land in financial hot water – as a friend of mine in the financial services industry, let's call her Helen, discovered the hard way. Helen was promoted to a very responsible new job: it was important to her to 'look the part', and she wanted to enjoy the trappings of her success right away. Even before she received her new pay cheque, she had bought lots of new clothes 'appropriate' for her new position. Helen's first shock came when she discovered that her after-tax income was substantially less than she thought it would be. The second shock came with the arrival of her credit card bills: she had racked up a huge amount of high-interest debt. The third shock came when her company suddenly downsized. She lost her new job, but still had to carry that enormous debt. Helen's fourth and final shock came when the debt-collectors started to call her at all hours, seeking payment. As things got worse, she retreated behind the silence of answering machines and Caller-I.D., until even friends like me couldn't reach her. Helen eventually found a new job and paid off the credit card companies, but it took months. Now she is careful. She has learned the cost of keeping up appearances, and she doesn't spend her future income before it's in her bank account.

Whether you are up to your ears in debt, or have just a few outstanding loans, the best thing you can do is to use any savings you have – other than that cushion for emergencies, or essentials such as food, rent and insurance – and pay off your loans.

If you are carrying several different kinds of debt, pay off the loan with the highest interest rate first. That is, if your credit card has a rate of 15 per cent, your car loan a rate of 12 per cent, and your student loan a rate of 10 per cent, then pay off your *entire* credit card debt first (and try shopping with cash instead of a card for a while), then work on the car loan, and finally the student loan.

Short-term debt can be a useful financial tool, but carrying long-term, high-interest debt can be a destructive force in your life. The only time it makes sense *not* to pay off your loans in full is when you are charged a lower interest rate on your debt – your student loan, for example – than the interest you can receive on a savings account or another type of investment.

OWN YOUR OWN HOME

In Britain, buying property may be the most popular way to invest and grow money. At every cocktail party or social occasion, the main topic of conversation is invariably the value of property. In fact, people probably check the price of comparable home sales more frequently than they check stock market prices. In some areas, house values are increasing by 30 per cent a year and doubling in five years or less. These bonanzas make news, of course, and these are the stories you always hear about. Meanwhile, in other areas, prices are barely moving or have historically gone down. Those whose property values increased greatly in the early 1980s experienced an equally precipitous decline a decade or so later. Property owners seem to have a short memory when it comes to market downturns, but there is always a risk of a prolonged slump.

Property is often the largest single investment people make in their lives. And because of all the emotions associated with owning a home, many people don't think through this huge expenditure as clearly as they do other kinds of investments. But they should. It's near heresy in the UK to suggest that buying property may *not* be the best investment for some people, and that renting might be better value. But I'll say it all the same: you should think very carefully before committing yourself to buying a home.

When most of my friends bought property in the mid-1980s, I continued to rent and save diligently for a deposit. Rather than join the stampede to buy any old flat simply because it was the thing to do, I consciously decided to wait and build up my reserves to buy a place I really wanted to live in. By the time the real estate market dropped in the early 1990s, I had saved enough to snap up a much larger apartment than I could have afforded a few years earlier.

Nonetheless, you may feel that you have reached a point in life where you simply want to own a home, or perhaps you've heard that monthly mortgage payments are cheaper than monthly rent, but are afraid that you cannot afford it. Well, the good news is that lenders are now twisting themselves into pretzels for the honour of lending you their money, and mortgages are the cheapest they've been since the 1950s.

The bad news is that many people are unrealistic about what they can afford.

Generally, you will need to put down a deposit, make monthly mortgage payments and cover many additional costs – such as legal fees, moving costs, survey fees, stamp duty, and insurance, among others. These expenses make home ownership more costly than you may assume. Finally, the great British sin is to over-decorate the first house, which you will live in on average for just five to seven years. My advice: make practical, not extraordinary, modifications to your first home – and save your money for the day when you settle down and buy the place of your dreams.

Try to save as much as you can before you buy a home, and delay buying until you've saved enough for a deposit. Don't pick out the wallpaper until you know exactly how much that new home is going to cost and how you are going to pay for it.

If you are sure that you want to buy a property right now, then you will probably need to get a mortgage. There are various types, but the central question is how you want to pay the loan back – bit by bit, as in a repayment mortgage, or all in one go at the end, as in an interest-only mortgage? Despite all of this gobbledy-gook, all mortgages boil down to one of these two types. Indeed, there are many schemes, and you will have to research which one makes the most sense for you.

Always put a deposit down. The bigger your deposit up-front, the smaller your repayments will be later. The best deals are for people who borrow only 75 or 80 per cent of the value of the property. If you need more than that, you may pay a higher interest rate and extra charges. If you can't afford a deposit, some lenders will offer you a 100 per cent mortgage. However, I think it's irresponsible to take out a 100 per cent mortgage, especially if you are a first-time home buyer. The assumption underlying this type of mortgage is that house prices will continue to rise strongly. But as we all know, the market is cyclical and a downturn is inevitable. If you get caught in a down market and are forced to sell, it will be extremely difficult – if not impossible – to recoup the purchase price of the property plus all of the interest you've paid. This is the part of the 100 per cent mortgage equation that people choose to ignore – at their peril.

A word of caution: before borrowing to the hilt, be honest with yourself about your *future* income and expenses – will your salary keep increasing? Do you plan on having children? (If so, that will mean a big drop in your spending ability.) Do you have a pension plan?

A mortgage, like other types of loan, is subject to interest: to minimise your costs, you should try to borrow as little money as possible and pay it back as quickly as possible. A rule of thumb is that you shouldn't spend more than 30 per cent of your take-home pay on your mortgage payments.

IT'S NEVER TOO EARLY TO START A PENSION

Do you find yourself saying the following words?:

- I'm too young to worry about contributing to a pension.
- Why bother to start a pension: I could die tomorrow.
- I don't have enough money to contribute to a pension.
- I'm too old now, so I'm going to let things take care of themselves.
- I know I should have a pension, but I can't decide which company to open one with.

If you say any of these things, then you have fallen into the *excuse trap* – as I did, all the way to my mid-thirties. I contributed only a small amount to my company pensions, but didn't come near to depositing the maximum that I could have, and I never monitored my pension schemes. I gave myself the 'immortality' excuse: I was so young and full of promise that I thought I was going to live forever. But in my mid-thirties, my body started to tell me that *it* wasn't going to survive for ever. The body that had once hussled and freaked into the early morning hours at New York's finest discos, now sought the plush comfort of an overstuffed club chair. The little aches and pains I began to notice were intimations of my advancing age, and I realised that if I continued making excuses I might find myself sipping a lukewarm cup of tea in a one-room bedsit, listening to old disco records, wondering what happened to all of my youthful promise. The need for a real pension plan became frighteningly apparent. I immediately shook my booty all the way to a financial planner.

You have to realise that because we are living longer these days, you might only have thirty years worth of earnings to pay for *more* than thirty years of retirement. Remember what retirement means: it means *not* earning. The only money you'll have to pay your bills when you retire is the money you save during your working years. Think of that, and then ask yourself: am I financially prepared for my non-earning retirement?

It's never too early to start planning for your retirement. As soon as you can afford to put away something in a pension scheme – even if it's only £10 a month – you should begin to do so.

If you are lucky enough to work for a company that has a pension plan, then you should join it immediately. Try to contribute the maximum amount. Most companies will add to your contributions and pay the set-up charges. If you take another job, you can still claim income from the first pension on your retirement, and you can also join your new employer's pension plan.

If you are a freelancer, or if your company doesn't have its own retirement scheme, then you should consider a personal pension plan. It lowers your taxable income: every pound you put into your plan is a deduction from your gross income. In effect, because the part of your income which you put into your pension is untaxed, the government is 'giving' you 23 pence for every one pound invested. The disadvantage is that personal pensions have high commissions and charges. After all, who else is going to look after you in your old age?

Other rules of thumb:

- If you are single, you definitely need a pension.
- Married couples need to think carefully about the type of pay-out they want to arrange. As romantic as it sounds, it is very rare that both spouses die at the same time; both of you need to participate in the planning of a pension and be aware of the details.
- As your financial circumstances improve, you should increase the amount you put away.
- You should monitor your returns to ensure they are on target. You should also monitor your overall investment to see if its growth is on target for the amount of money you want to retire with and for your planned retirement date. If your targets are not being met, you should think about investing in a different scheme.

The only way you will have something to live on in retirement is if you start contributing your money to a pension plan now; with proper forethought, you can incubate quite a lovely nest-egg for your dotage. But if all you contribute is excuses, then you know exactly what kind of interest you will be earning, and exactly what sort of bed-sit you will spend your golden years in.

INVEST TO GROW YOUR MONEY

For years I considered stocks the plague and stockbrokers the carriers of that plague. This is a very Depression-era view of the stock market, and, in truth, it wasn't based on anything more than my own ignorance. I ignored the stock market until I was in my early thirties, when I began to teach on Wall Street and learn how the markets actually work. As I began to understand the benefits of investing, I decided I should, in fact, invest some of my money. To make up for the years when I did nothing about planning for retirement, I invested part of my pension in stocks. After a few mistakes (which I'll discuss later) I came to see the real benefits of the market. Soon I was putting any income above and beyond what I had budgeted for daily living expenses and my savings into the stocks of high-quality companies. It has proven to be a rewarding experience, in many ways, and I only wish I had started to invest earlier.

Many British people use the words 'saving' and 'investing' interchangeably, but they are not the same thing. Saving means putting your money into something essentially risk-free, such as a building society account. Investing means putting your money into a product, such as stocks, bonds and unit trusts whose value will fluctuate, possibly risking the loss of your money. Investing should be a supplement to your savings, a way to boost the overall return of your money.

As a general rule of thumb, you should invest only after you have at least three to six months' worth of savings put away for emergencies, have your debts sorted, have the insurance coverage you need, have a retirement plan in place and – most importantly – can afford to *lose* the money you invest.

It would be nice to be a millionaire, don't you think? So how do you do it – win the lottery? Well, it could happen, but the chances of hitting the jackpot are fourteen million to one. How about marrying money? But then you have to pay in a different way. What about inheriting £999,999, putting it into a building society, and letting time and interest do the rest? Well, that option is available only for a precious few. But the best option for the rest of us is to invest your money in stocks or bonds – which, contrary to popular opinion, is not the absolute equivalent of gambling. We Americans love to invest in stocks, bonds and gilts (which we call government bonds) and we have learned that the key to success is to concentrate on quality companies with proven, long-term track records. You have a choice of two kinds of investment:

- When you buy a share of *stock*, you become the owner of a fraction of that company and have the right to share in that company's profits and future growth.
- When you buy a *bond* you are making a loan to a company, institution or government entity that promises to pay you interest at regular intervals and to repay the full loan at a future date.

Historically, stocks and bonds have tended to earn higher returns over longer periods of time than ultra-safe building society or bank savings accounts. But investing *is* a risk. Risk can bring reward, but it can also bring loss. Only you can decide how much risk you're willing to take for the chance to earn higher returns.

One common approach to spreading your risk is to invest about half of your assets in stocks, one-third in bonds or gilts and the remainder in something safe, like a building society account.

If you are interested in investments, but don't want to make a decision about individual stocks and bonds, or don't have enough money to properly spread the risk (£50,000 is a general benchmark), consider buying shares in a *unit trust* or *investment trust*. In this type of investment, thousands of people with the same investment objective pool their money; a manager or team of managers then invests the sum in a variety of stocks, bonds or other market instruments. In general, stock funds are riskier than bond funds, but they have also provided a higher return over the years.

PROTECT YOUR ASSETS

For most people, insurance is a dreadful topic – it's confusing and expensive, and it has connotations of sickness, disaster, theft and death. No wonder most people would prefer not to talk about it, or even to think about it. But those same factors are precisely why you need to plan ahead, so that you will not have to worry about bankrupting your family while coping with some unforeseen crisis.

Life assurance
If you have a family or other dependants, life assurance will provide a certain amount of financial cover should you die. It is an important and relatively inexpensive investment to make – even if you plan on living for hundreds of years. One of the most popular forms of life assurance is *term assurance*, the policy for which lasts for a fixed term – say, ten years – providing a fixed amount of coverage – say, £250,000. If you're single, life assurance is a waste of money; but it is *essential* if you have dependants.

Health insurance
There are three main types of insurance which provide coverage when you are ill or disabled:

- *Critical illness insurance* will pay out a lump sum if you are diagnosed with one of a number of specific illnesses, such as cancer, heart disease or kidney failure.
- *Permanent health insurance* will pay out 65–75 per cent of your salary if you are made redundant or become sick or injured. While most large companies offer disability coverage to their employees, those who work for smaller companies or freelance are left to fend for themselves.

- *Private Medical insurance* will pay your medical expenses if you become ill and want private, or specialised care. If you are satisfied with your NHS care, this type of insurance may not be necessary.

Permanent Protection insurance will continue to pay money to you for a short period of time should you fall sick or lose your job. But it's expensive and comes with a lot of caveats. Check to see what is excluded from your coverage, and that you have worked long enough to qualify. If you're self-employed, it is extremely difficult to claim on this type of policy, so don't bother with it.

A *will* provides further protection for your family wealth. I have seen families practically destroy themselves over the division of an inheritance, and the larger the inheritance the nastier the fight – after all, that story-line has been the basis for many parables, Shakespearean plays and Los Angeleno melodramas over the ages. While there are basic rules in the UK on who gets what if you die intestate (without a will), they are *very* basic. Your money doesn't necessarily go to whom you think it will; it can go right to the State. If you want to ensure that the people you care about inherit the assets you care about, then I suggest you have a will drawn up professionally.

Money is an integral part of our lives from the cradle to the grave. We hope our ability to deal with it improves as we mature, but unfortunately that doesn't always happen. Some people get caught in a time-warp, and seek to have someone else pay for everything – as their parents did for years. Others get stuck in bad habits and stubbornly refuse to change their ways. They seem to view their bad habit as an entitlement: they don't want to abdicate control of their finances, yet they repeat the same mistakes over and over again; they say they 'can't deal with change' and remain wilfully ignorant. And then there are those who believe they can shape their financial destiny to fit any dream they might have, despite what the actual numbers on their bank statements might say.

Most of us are responsible with money but continue to struggle with some form of these weaknesses all our lives. Sometimes our financial problems seem merely the equivalent of a bad-hair day; at other times they can take on epic dimensions, and we find ourselves struggling with money like Laocoon with the giant serpents. It is from the struggle, however, that we gain experience, confidence and insight. The key is to learn to identify your own demons and work to defeat them.

The essential advice of this book, then, is that you must learn personal financial responsibility. As Billie Holiday sang, 'Mamma may have, Papa may have, but God bless the child that's got his own!'

CHAPTER 2

GAZING INTO THE FINANCIAL MIRROR: HOW DO YOU SPEND?

The Alvin Hall Quick Quiz on Spending

- Do you spend every pound you earn – and then some?
- Does the word 'Sale' in a shop window act on you like an aphrodisiac?
- Does the sight of higher numbers in your current account bring on an urge to spend, spend, spend?
- Do your purchases just seem to happen, or do you plan ahead before going shopping?
- Do you have clothes in your wardrobe that you haven't worn more than once?
- Do you ignore your bills, or file them in places where you don't have to look at them?
- Does it require considerable effort to lay your hands on a specific credit card bill?
- Do you take a taxi when you could walk or take public transport?
- Do you order take-away when you could cook at home?
- Do you find yourself tapping into your overdraft every month? Do you know what that habit costs you?

If you answer 'Yes' to five or more of the above, then you are in need of spending therapy. To learn the importance of spending your money wisely – and some easy ways to improve your spending habits – read on.

'*Who Are We, Where Did We Come From, Where Are We Going?*' is the title of one of the most haunting paintings by the Post-Impressionist artist Paul Gauguin. In search of happiness, in 1891 Gauguin abandoned his family and career as a stockbroker in Paris to live and paint in the Pacific-island paradise of Tahiti.

While you may not require the drastic change in life that Gauguin did, you can probably understand his desire to live on a beautiful tropical island. You surely have dreams and aspirations of your own.

But how frustrating it is when your dreams confront the reality of your pay cheque. Many people find that most or all of their income has been used up before the month's end. They have little idea where their money has gone, and the suggestion that they should set aside anything for the future seems like the last unnecessary cruelty. Indeed, it is easier than ever to spend your money today, faster than ever, whether you are rich or poor. You turn on the television, try to shop for bargains or have a pint at your local, and what do you see? *Temptation!*, as my Uncle Son used to thunder with Baptist fervour. *Temptation everywhere!*

We all fritter money away. I spend too much on magazines. Perhaps you have a daily chocolate bar or cappuccino. For others it might be cigarettes or lottery tickets, the impulse buys at the chemist's, the extra collectible at a car-boot sale. Yet spending more than you can afford, like eating a whole pint of ice cream by yourself, will not buy you happiness. More likely, it will keep you up at night.

For many people, money is like an aphrodisiac and spending it comes as an orgasmic release. It's as if earning the money isn't enough; that ratification of success only comes in *spending* it. It is much more satisfying, after all, to buy an object of (formerly forbidden) desire – a trophy, in effect – than to do the smart thing and save your money for an abstract future. The feeling behind this orgasmic spending seems to be: 'I've worked for it, and now I want the gratification of spending it, so get out of the way.'

I understand this impulse, because from time to time I have felt this way – and continue to feel this way – myself. So what's the solution? The key is to learn not to give in to that primal urge to spend your money as soon as you get it (or before). This is harder than it sounds, but I have two suggestions on how you can trick yourself into good habits.

First, keep yourself out of harm's way. If I have a windfall, for example, I *know* that I will succumb to the enticements of aesthetically pleasing material goods. So I simply won't let myself walk through the Valley of the Shadows of Temptation. I go to a museum or for a walk in the park rather than anywhere near an art gallery, antique store, or favourite clothing shop. If this sounds easy, just try it – and stick to it.

Second, try the old placebo trick. If my craving to buy something overwhelms me, or I feel I deserve a treat, I will sometimes allow myself a small substitute purchase in place of an ecstatic blow-out. Recently, for example, I had a large speaking fee burning a hole in my pocket. I was tempted to buy a very expensive pair of cufflinks, but managed to limit myself to a unique, yet modestly-priced pair of alternative cufflinks. The spending mania passed, and I had the satisfaction of buying something I wanted at less than one-fifth the price I had been sorely tempted to spend.

If you are serious about developing healthy financial habits, then you need to recognise that shopping isn't therapy, and that you won't find lasting satisfaction at the end of a credit card receipt. It's a lesson many of us take years to learn.

First, you must take stock of where you are right now. Look unflinchingly into your financial mirror, and ask yourself, *à la* Gauguin: 'Who am I as a spender and saver? Where did I come from financially? Where do I want my money to take me?'

Second, you must get organised. Begin by setting a budget and establishing long-term goals. Then set about taking the necessary steps to turn your dreams into concrete realities – and give yourself a few sweet payoffs along the way as you achieve some pre-set targets.

HOW DOES MONEY FLOW THROUGH YOUR FINGERS?

Like most people, I was never taught the basics of personal finance. As a kid on the farm, I didn't know how to reconcile a bank account. As a student, buying a stock was the furthest thing from my mind. After graduating from university, I worked for several years in the American South, and had a tendency to overspend on things I thought defined me as a man of good taste. In retrospect, I see that I was making the same mistakes over and over again, only in different ways.

Then I moved to New York City – one of the most expensive places on Earth – to get started in a career on Wall Street. Before moving to the Big Apple, I had lived from one pay cheque to the next, but I had always been able to cover my expenses. Now, suddenly, I discovered that I was spending far more than I could afford. Where did it all go? My earnings seemed to be leaking through my fingers, month after month, year after year. What was

I doing wrong? I didn't consider myself a wasteful spender, but I had some sneaking suspicions about my habits.

To find out exactly how I was spending my money, I fell back on my self-discipline: As I mentioned in Chapter 1, I kept a financial diary for one month. I wrote down every expenditure, trying to use exact figures as much as possible – which was easy for regular bills, such as mortgage payments – and guesstimating the rest. I went over bank account statements, old bills and credit card statements, and I collected receipts from stores, petrol stations, dry cleaners and restaurants. At the end of the month I studied the figures.

To my surprise, I discovered that my food shopping bills were reasonable and consistent (I always shop for food with cash, the same amount every time, and I always bring a shopping list and stick to it). To my chagrin, however, I discovered that I was spending a lot of money on dinners with friends at restaurants, on magazines and clothes. The financial diary had made it clear to me just where my money was going, and I vowed to change my profligate ways.

Recognising my bad habits was one thing, but actually changing them was another. You've got to learn how to discipline yourself, and for most people this *will* be a struggle.

TAKE A HARD LOOK IN THE FINANCIAL MIRROR: WHAT DO YOU SEE?

When you ask, 'Mirror, mirror on the wall, who is the financially fairest of them all?' which of these will be your answer?

- 'Me, of course.' Some people see in the mirror what they want to see. They believe they have healthy financial habits, no matter what the truth is. They may see the truth only after the mirror cracks – which may be too late.

- 'Not me – I'm only a rabbit in the headlights.' Others are scared stiff by the mere thought of money. Perhaps what they see in the mirror is the prospect of eternal poverty, so they save and save and forget to enjoy life. They need to learn how to be more generous with themselves.

- 'Not me – right at the moment. But let me get to work and I'll be the fairest one day soon.' These people are honest about their financial situation and are ready to take action.

If you feel comfortably knowledgeable about your income and outgoings, then maybe you can skip this section. But if, like most people, you're only vaguely aware of what's in your bank account, if you feel as though you barely make it from one payday to the next, or if you're annoyed that others seem to be sprinting ahead in life while you drag along like a snail, then take a fiscal inventory. Take an honest look at your income and how you spend it. Is your money going towards building the life of your dreams? Or does it somehow leak through your fingers month after month, leaving you no better off?

To find out where your money is really going, fill out the Budget Worksheet on pages 36–37.

There is a wide stylistic difference in the ways people use their money. At one extreme of the spending spectrum are the worry-warts – the people who constantly fret about every aspect of their money and obsess over accounting details. These are often older people who have lived through financial hardship; they are worried they will end their lives in poverty. It's prudent to save and spend wisely, of course, but some of these folks risk becoming lonely and mean. They need to lighten up, spend more of their money while they can, and enjoy the fruits of their carefully managed lives. There is more to life than hoarding money, after all.

Budget Worksheet: Where does your money really go?

These are typical categories of income and expenditure that you should consider. At the beginning of the year, try to estimate what you think each category will cost you. At the end of the year, go back and note your actual costs. Then use what you've learned to plan a realistic budget for the future.

INCOME	TOTAL FOR YEAR	
	Estimated	*Actual*
Bonuses	£_____	_____
Dividends, capital gains, interest	_____	_____
Take-home pay	_____	_____
Other	_____	_____
EXPENDITURES		
Buildings insurance	£_____	_____
Car insurance	_____	_____
Clothing and footwear	_____	_____
Council tax	_____	_____
Water rates	_____	_____
Eating Out	_____	_____
Food and non-alcoholic drinks	_____	_____
Ground rent	_____	_____
Heating and lighting	_____	_____
Telephone bills	_____	_____
Holidays	_____	_____
Home contents insurance	_____	_____

Home – mortgage/rent

Home repairs and maintenance

Household goods –
  furniture, appliances

Income Tax payments

Leisure in (video hire, books,
  music, toys and hobbies)

Leisure out
  (e.g. cinema, theatre, sport)

Life assurance

Magazines and newspapers

Medical insurance

National Insurance contribution

Pension

Personal goods and services

Petrol

Public transport travel expenses

Repayment of loans

Road tax

Savings and investments

Service charges

Tobacco and alcohol

TV licence and TV subscriptions

SUMMARY

Total Income: £_____

Minus total expenditures: £_____

Your surplus or deficit: £_____

At the other end of the spectrum are the spendthrifts (and there are a lot more of these than the worry-warts). These are the type of people – many of them young and clueless – who take a *laissez-faire* or apathetic approach to money: they spend because they have money now, and worry little about the future. A few of them may even become addicted to spending. But if their habits are not checked over time, they have a good chance of finding themselves in a bind: with insufficient assets when they need them most, such as in an emergency or when they'd like to buy a house or shackled with heavy consumer debt, which can lead to sleepless nights, strife among friends and family, and even serious health problems.

If you are in this category, you may be in denial about the realities of life. Unexpected sickness, or other disasters? They don't happen to people like you. Sudden loss of income? Nah, never – that's for others to worry about. Plan for retirement? It's a long way off, or it's too late, or you can't be bothered. Right? But the problem with such delusions, delays and day dreams is that with time they will get the better of an imperfect human and make a fool out of him or her.

Most people fall into the middle ground between the worry-warts and the spendthrifts, or perhaps vacillate from one extreme to the other, regretting it all the way.

We all need to find that happy balance between meanness and spendthriftiness, or denial and satisfaction; it's what tennis players call the 'sweet spot' on a racquet, and it feels good when you hit it. If I were Harry Potter, I'd give everyone their own individual formula for Sweet Spot Tea. But, alas, I am no wizard, and it's up to you to do the hard work.

To achieve a healthy balance between income and expenditure, you must acknowledge your temptations and learn to control your impulses. Plan clearly for the future before you spend lavishly in the present.

- You must have a budget – whether in writing or in your mind's eye – which will give you a framework for your spending.
- When entering situations where your temptations are likely to overpower your will – in a supermarket, sweet shop or department store, for example – take only a limited amount of cash.
- Force yourself to save. Remember the words of jazz pianist Eubie Blake, who said he'd have taken much better care of himself if he'd known he was going to live for so long.

SET A BUDGET – AND STICK TO IT LIKE 'WHITE ON RICE'

Once you know how and where you're spending money, you *must* set a budget for yourself. It's the only way to know your boundaries and prepare for the future; without a budget, you are almost guaranteeing you will repeat past mistakes and get into financial trouble.

My friend Tom, a banker, has always been a very orderly person, and his wife Cindy used to chide him for being so anal about their restricted household budget. She'd mock his computer printouts, groan at his neat columns of numbers and roll her eyes when he asked for her shopping receipts. He'd just grin, and nod, and remind her to stick to the spending plan. As their income increased, so did the amount Tom allocated to saving, investing, mortgage payments, gifts, vacations and – most of all – their joint retirement account. While Cindy chafed at his rules, he had a long-range goal in mind. On their tenth wedding anniversary, he surprised Cindy by giving her an enormous diamond ring. Then, aged forty-six, he retired to a very comfortable life in their dream house by the sea. Who had the last laugh?

*   *   *

How do you get started on a budget? Discard sloppy guesswork or doe-eyed fantasising, check your records, write down a realistic projection of your income and expenses, carefully work out a spending plan and force yourself to stick to it.

In the early phases it will be tough going. But then, like a pianist practising the same *étude* over and over, sticking to your budget will become second nature. You'll know you've reached this point when you are shopping and intuitively sense when you are approaching your spending limits – even if your budget is not physically in front of you.

ALVIN HALL'S TEN FAVOURITE COMMON-SENSE TIPS FOR SENSIBLE SPENDING

1) Keep an honest diary of your daily expenses for just one month, and track how money *really* flows through your hands. It sounds tedious, but it's not so hard. It's a very useful and insightful exercise. The more you learn about your spending (no matter how painful), the more you will know where you must exercise self-control.

2) Always have a mental picture of your budget in mind, and use it like a compass that tells you where you are in relation to your ideal numbers.

Budget yourself to spend, say, £500 every month, and treat it like a draw-down account: every time you write a cheque, spend cash or use a credit card, round the expense *up* to the nearest whole number (thus, think of £29.30 as £30); subtract this figure from the total amount.

Arrange each category, or line item, in your budget

in a hierarchy of importance. If you own a house or flat, for example, your mortgage payments should be one of your top priorities.

Put in a line-item for 'fun' things such as holidays, after-Christmas sales and meals out for special occasions – or, as I do, for buying photographic art. Won't your holiday be much more enjoyable if you know you won't be paying for it long after your tan has faded?

3) Don't ignore your financial statements. Your bills may seem boring, or scary, but chucking them in the bin won't make them go away. It isn't boring, or uncool, to know what is happening with your money; on the contrary, running away from responsibility is immature. To commit yourself to taking charge of your finances is to become mature and empowered.

Always look at the interest expense on your debt. While you can't budget for it because it changes, you should be aware of it. It's very sobering to realise that your credit card debt alone can cost you more than some other, more important item on your budget.

Indeed, today you can periodically check your credit card balance – call the freephone number or go on-line – so you don't have to wait for your statement in the mail to know where you stand. You can get the picture on a daily basis.

4) If you are a freelancer or self-employed, budget for taxes. It's one of those areas people hate to think about, but ignore at their own peril. You can be sure the Inland Revenue won't forget that it is owed money, and it can make your life miserable at tax time. A good way to do this is to establish an interest-bearing

account, and make payments into it from every payment you receive.

5) Periodically, leave your credit card at home and shop
with cash instead. It's a lot harder to hand over a big
pile of cash than a little piece of plastic. Think of it like
Lent, where you vow to give up something enjoyable
for a time as a bit of spiritual discipline. (But you don't
have to be absolutist about this: if you use your credit
card for business expenses, and you know you will be
reimbursed, that's different from using plastic for fun
and games.)

6) Avoid impulse buying. Allow yourself to go shopping
only one day a week, and limit your purchases to
necessities. *Don't*, for example, buy five pairs of nearly-
identical black trousers. *Do* try on clothes before
purchasing them. Make yourself wait at least twenty-
four hours before buying an expensive item to make
sure you really want it.

7) Remember the old adage: 'Don't shop for food when
you are hungry, for it will only increase your appetite
and the amount you spend.' Make a shopping list
before leaving the house, and stick to it once you
are in the store. By extension, don't buy clothes when
you are feeling needy.

8) Limit your nights out each week, and this includes
weekends. Keep track of your tab; do not simply lay
your credit card down on the bar and get blind drunk
as quickly as possible. Look at the bar bill in the
morning.

9) Watch how much money you spend on snacks. Take-away is more expensive than you think, while making dinner for yourself at home is cheaper and more fun than you might imagine.

10) To translate your financial fantasies – a new car, a pet goldfish, a skiing holiday – into achievable realities, make a reasonable 'wish-list' of goals, and assign them a pounds and pence value. Such a list may reveal that your goals are within reach, or it may scare you and force you to reprioritise. In any event, it will give you a clear picture of the costs of your dreams. Then start saving.

GET ORGANISED

We live in the era of junk-mail overload. Our postboxes seem to be overflowing with solicitations, catalogues, magazines and, of course, bills. Do you ever suspect the paper is procreating at night?

The temptation is to pretend those bills don't exist. But ignoring them won't make them go away – if anything, it will only make your next bill larger, and encourage the stores and credit card companies to send you *more* mail, filled with increasingly angry messages asking for their money, please, now.

The answer is to get organised.

I hate to break the news to those of you who are neatness-challenged, but it's a lot easier to put your financial life in order if you know where all of your papers are.

In an ideal world, you should file your important paperwork as soon as you receive it. But the next best thing is to get yourself an 'in-box' where you store papers that need to be filed, and to do a filing once every week. Pick a night when you are doing nothing else, so that you can concentrate and get it over with quickly. Then purse your lips and sip from that glass of chilled Chardonnay.

The simplest way to keep your paperwork under control is to create a number of files and keep them in a filing cabinet – even if it's only a cardboard one. Keep your files as simple as possible.

Here are a few suggestions for the kinds of file you may want to create:

- Bills to be paid – for electric, heat, telephone charges that need to be paid straight away. You could file these individually, or under 'utilities', or some other name if you prefer
- Brokerage accounts – keep statements and certificates
- Car – for purchase agreement, title, warranty, repair work; you may need a separate file for your car loan, if you have one
- Current account and savings account statements
- Computer-related items – receipts, instruction booklets, etc.
- Correspondence – personal and business
- Credit cards – each card should have its own folder for receipts and the original credit card agreements
- Home – for all documents relating to purchase and general expenses; create a separate file for Home Improvements, to track those specific expenses
- Insurance – for policies, record of claims, etc.
- Mortgage – for interest-payment statements
- Pay cheque – keep pay-stubs, and any written information about your salary
- Pension/Retirement plan – save descriptions and explanations of the plan, statements, and other documents
- Personal papers – including birth certificate, passport, university degree certificates, marriage certificate, etc. (A

will should be kept in a very safe place that is fire and flood proof)

- Receipts – if you really want to see where your money is going, this can be a very useful file
- Student loans – keep any documentation about the loan agreement, and your statements
- Taxes – filing statements and records
- Warranties and user manuals for appliances

Another useful tool is the computer. More and more people are using personal finance software to get a clear sense of how they are spending their money. These programs will automatically reconcile your account, and categorise your expenditures into headings such as 'clothes', 'housing' and 'telephone'. At the end of a few months, you can see how much you have spent on, say, restaurant dinners in the winter versus the summer. As long as you are honest when you type in your figures, this is a very good way to look into the financial mirror. A useful feature of these programs is a worksheet that allows you to figure out what your payments would be on a loan, or how much you will need to save monthly or annually at a given interest rate to accumulate a certain amount of money.

Does reining-in your spending sound like a bore or the death of good times? It really isn't. At the end of the day, it's more fun to buy things you truly want, and can afford, than tossing and turning all night, worrying about how to pay your bills.

Tips on Wise Spending

We all have to spend to survive, of course; it's just a question of how we choose to do it – carelessly or wisely. Here are a few common-sense tips on wise spending:

- Spend today *only* what you can afford today. How do you know what that is? Create a budget. That is, calculate what you are spending now; figure how much you'd like to be saving every month; take a deep breath, and decide where to cut your present spending.

    Another way to do this is to start with a clean slate. Forget what your current spending is, and ask yourself how much you'd *like* to be spending on each category in your budget. Be practical.

- Avoid wasting your money on high-priced brand-name products when lesser, or generic, equivalents will do. A 60p can of name-brand baked beans purchased at the corner shop does not necessarily taste any better than a supermarket's own brand you can get down the street.

- Eat out less, and drink less alcohol. Having fewer drinks can certainly lower the cost of eating out. Vegetarian, pasta or rice dishes generally cost less than meat-based entrées.

- Move to a cheaper flat, consider sharing a space, or even buying a home rather than renting. We'll discuss this more in Chapter 5, but purchasing your own home can, in the long run, prove less costly than renting.

- Use public transport, a bicycle, a skateboard, or your feet rather than your car. Cars are a nice luxury, but they aren't always necessary, particularly in a large city.

- When buying clothes, don't chase fashion. Buy classic clothing that will last and look good for years. Minimise your accessories and limit yourself to one or at most two of everything. Anything that requires dry cleaning will cost you more over the long term.

While accessories such as jewellery, lotions and make-up make you feel better, you should ask yourself how many of those things you *really* need. Isn't one, or at most two, bottles of perfume enough? And what else could you have done with all the cash you spent on such luxuries?

- Prioritise your fun, and limit your entertainment budget. Unfortunately, part of growing up is realising you can't have, or do, it all.

- Do sit-ups at home, go for a run in the park or bicycle to work rather than pay for a health-club membership.

- Plan your vacations carefully. Taking a holiday is wonderful and healthy, but make sure that you stick to a plan and budget, or you won't feel relaxed once you return home and have to face your bills.

  Consider going to closer, less popular destinations, in the off-season.

- Do your homework before you buy – especially on big-ticket items. This point is not as obvious as it might appear to be.

  The more research you do before making a purchase, the more you will know about the product and the more intelligent your purchasing decision will be. For example, paying a high price is not a guarantee that you will get high quality, nor does paying a low price. You need to focus on *total* costs over the long term. A cheap car is not necessarily more fuel-efficient, or less expensive to maintain, than a slightly more expensive one; indeed, the cheaper car could cost you more in maintenance over the long term than the more expensive one.

CHAPTER 3

DEBT IN THE AGE
OF INSTANT GRATIFICATION

The Alvin Hall Quick Quiz on Debt

- Does it bother you to carry debt from month to month?
- Do you have more money in savings than you owe on your credit cards?
- Have you ever left your credit card at home *on purpose*, and gone shopping only with cash?
- Do you have no more than three credit and/or store cards?
- Do you have a clear idea how much your consumer debt is costing you each month?
- Have you ever said 'No' when a bank has offered to increase your credit limit?

If you answered 'Yes' to four or more of these questions, then you have good fundamental debt practices. If not, you need to pay more attention to your plastic habit – the number-one cause of excessive spending.

'**T**he safest road to hell is the gradual one – the gentle slope, soft underfoot, without sudden turnings, without milestones, without signposts,' C.S. Lewis cautioned. Replace the word 'hell' with 'debt' or 'bankruptcy', and you sum up the way many of us sink slowly and comfortably into bad financial habits – especially overspending with credit cards.

It's possible to become addicted to spending in the same way that people become addicted to alcohol, tobacco, TV, chocolate and sex . . . or so many people believe in the States. Psychologists have identified a number of causes for this (such as the way your parents handled *their* finances), and have begun to study the problem, but it remains a huge issue for many.

Indeed, it is sobering to learn that in Britain today, the total amount of outstanding consumer debt on credit cards is some £13 billion!

I once had a bad plastic habit myself (and for a man who doesn't wear Polyester this was ironic). And so I know, from hard personal experience, how difficult it can be to stop piling debt on top of debt, until you get in too deep.

In the 1970s, when I was teaching English in Miami, Florida, I drove a snappy Mazda RX-3 and carried twenty-nine credit cards in my wallet. Most of these cards were from petrol stations and department stores up and down the eastern seaboard, and most of them had very low limits, usually only $300–500 (£200–350).

Debt in the UK

Of course, I am not alone in finding debt a thorny problem. Personal debt is a major problem for thousands of people in the UK today. Just consider these statistics:

- The amount of outstanding consumer credit in 1999 – £115.2 billion – is equivalent to over £1,900 per UK citizen.
- In 1999, there was 115,416 court summonses for debt of between £5,000 and £25,000 by the county courts of England and Wales.
- During the period from 1997–1999, there were 96,620 properties repossessed.

It's important that you understand how debt works so that you can avoid it, or get rid of it as quickly as possible.

Twenty-nine credit cards! It seems absolutely insane to me now, but at the time it made perfect sense. Having a wallet full of cards was a source of both comfort and independence for me (a weird psychological combination, I know), and I charged everything from petrol to my boxer shorts on them. I even charged the flowers I bought each week for my apartment. A wallet full of plastic said to me: I am a successful adult. In an odd way, the approval I received from these big credit card companies made me feel as if my accomplishments had been ratified by society – until, that is, I suddenly realised that I was in debt from Maine to Florida.

The problem was that, as a teacher, I wasn't earning enough to cover my bills. In fact, I was spending more than I was making, and became a veritable poster boy for the neediness that credit card companies tap into.

Then came the inevitable day when I realised I couldn't even cover the minimum payments due on my credit card debt. I had gone a step too far. And I was not so in need of approval that I failed to recognise this as a very clear warning sign. I considered seeking professional help from a credit counselling service, but in Miami there was none available at the time. After giving it a little more thought, I decided on my own self-help plan: I'd get a single major bank card, with a reasonable limit, and consolidate the debt from most of my other cards on to the new card.

Then I got tough with myself. After neatly arranging my twenty-nine credit cards and their statements up and down my dining-room table – like a hand of Solitaire – I went through them and decided which I could get rid of and which I needed to keep. I called up the credit card companies and negotiated a couple of months' grace period for my debts and wrote up a strict spending budget for myself. Then I took out the scissors, cut up the cards I had cancelled and threw them away. This wasn't an easy thing to do for a recovering plastic addict – I didn't even drink then! – but it was long overdue.

For the next year, I did not allow myself to use a single credit card, and eventually my austerity plan worked: I paid off my high-interest debt, and even managed to save some money. To make sure I wouldn't relapse, I bought a wallet that had room for only three cards. (I still use the same kind of wallet today.)

Judging from this story, you may think I believe that credit cards are inherently evil. But I don't. Looking back, I see that while I was tempted to blame the credit card companies for my debt, in reality the problem was *me*. After all, I did not have to accept the credit card offers that magically appeared in my mail.

Today, I carry just three credit cards, and use them judiciously. I have learned enough about debt to know that I never, ever want to be over my head in debt again. Just as I grew to understand the psychological need for approval that drove me to use my credit cards irresponsibly, so I gained the ability to control myself.

THE NATURE OF THE BEAST

Debt is a problem that many of us are more intimate with than we'd care to admit, yet we don't fully understand it. There is 'good' debt, and 'bad' debt. Do you know the difference?

Debt that is considered 'good' is money invested in yourself and your future – such as money used to buy property, or borrowed for education or to help start up a business.

'Bad' debt, commonly referred to as 'consumer debt', is money borrowed for short-term, perishable pleasures, such as shopping sprees, lavish dinners and expensive vacations. One thing that makes consumer debt so 'bad' is that it almost always comes with a high interest rate, which can really hurt you over time. For example, consider this scary fact: if you earn £17,000 a year, and have £30,000 in combined store and credit card debt, then you will never be able to pay off your debt in your lifetime if you make only the minimum payments each month.

Hence this inflexible rule: if you have savings, you should pay off your high-interest-rate debt – such as that from store cards, credit cards and car loans – as quickly as possible, and before you pay your lower-interest debt, such as your mortgage or school loans.

Let's say you have £5,000 in a savings account, earning 6 per cent interest. At the same time, you are carrying a credit card debt of £7,000, at 15 per cent interest. While it might make you feel secure to have your £5,000 in savings, it's a false security, for you are losing money faster than you earn it due to the high interest on your debt.

The wisdom gleaned from this example is numerically straight-forward, but emotionally difficult: *don't* fall into the trap of false economy; *do* use at least some of your savings to aggressively pay off your high-interest debts.

PLASTIC: IS IT FANTASTIC?

The modern credit card was first introduced by the Bank of America, in Fresno, California, in 1958. Today, 'plastic' is a wonderfully convenient way to pay for almost everything – from Marmite to movie tickets or a pack of Marlboro Lights – almost anywhere in the world.

If you pay your bill *in full*, and *on time*, *every month*, then plastic is, indeed, fantastic. It offers you a short-term, interest-free loan; it allows you to go shopping without the hassle of carrying cash; it lists all your charges on one convenient statement; it is helpful in emergencies, such as when your car breaks down; it allows you to earn free airmiles while you shop; it often guarantees you the lowest price on a purchase, and allows you to return an item should the merchandise be defective.

There are literally dozens of credit cards issued by different companies to choose from. You need to shop around for one that best suits you. If you tend to carry a balance from month to month, for example, you should find a card with the lowest interest rate possible. If you pay your balance on time, however, you should look for a card that doesn't charge an annual fee.

It's relatively simple to find the information you need. Call the banks and ask whether they are having any credit card promotions. Ask what the interest rate is and the duration of that rate. Be aware of short-term 'teaser' rates, designed to entice new customers, which usually last from three to nine months and are then replaced by much higher, permanent rates. Ask how much the on-going interest charge will be after the teaser rate ends, and what the annual fee, if any, will be. Then select the card that makes the most sense for you.

The dirty little secret about credit card shopping – a secret that many Americans know very well – is to negotiate the best deal by playing one bank off another. Remind bank A, which offers rate

Debtor's Anonymous Self-quiz

If your spending becomes chronic, it can wreak havoc on your personal life, and even your health. You may want to consult an expert about ways to stop. In the US, Debtors Anonymous (DA) is a non-profit organisation modelled on Alcoholics Anonymous (AA), which provides support to people trying to break their debt habit.

Below is a DA questionnaire to help determine whether you are a chronic debtor. If you answer 'Yes' to eight or more of the following questions you may have a compulsive habit, and should seek help:

- Are your debts making your home life unhappy?
- Does the pressure of your debts distract you from your daily work?
- Are your debts affecting your reputation?
- Do your debts cause you to think less of yourself?
- Have you ever given false information in order to obtain credit?
- Have you ever made unrealistic promises to your creditors?
- Does the pressure of your debts make you careless of the welfare of your family?
- Do you ever fear that your employer, family or friends will learn the extent of your total indebtedness?
- When faced with a difficult financial situation, does the prospect of borrowing give you an inordinate feeling of relief?
- Does the pressure of your debts cause you to have difficulty sleeping?
- Has the pressure of your debts ever caused you to consider getting drunk?

- Have you ever borrowed money without giving adequate consideration to the rate of interest you are required to pay?
- Do you usually expect a negative response when you are subject to a credit investigation?
- Have you ever developed a strict regimen for paying off your debts, only to break it under pressure?
- Do you justify your debts by telling yourself that you are superior to the 'other' people, and when you get your 'break' you'll be out of debt?

X, that bank B has offered rate Y, for the new year; then ask bank A if they will meet, or better, rate Y. You might be surprised to see how effective this tactic can be.

On the other hand, credit cards make it almost *too* easy to spend money. We've all been in that situation where even if we really don't want to spend any more, the object in front of us is so beautiful, so perfect and such a bargain, that consumer lust overwhelms our reason. Before we realise what has happened, we've laid our card across the counter, and can only stand by helplessly watching as it is ravaged before our eyes.

Indeed, despite what you might want to believe, a wallet full of plastic is not a sign of financial strength, sophistication or security. If you keep charging on your card, make only the minimum monthly payment and carry your high-interest debt from month to month, then credit cards will prove to be debilitating to your financial health.

One of the most misunderstood aspects of credit cards is the *grace period* – the time (typically three to four weeks) between your purchase and when you receive your bill – when a credit card company does not charge you interest. If you pay off your debt in full by the due date, then no interest accrues on new purchases because they are subject to the grace period. If you don't pay your balance in full every month, however, you are granted no grace period for your new charges: as soon as you make a purchase, interest on your debt begins to accrue *immediately*. It's a double hit that makes carrying a balance from month to month even more costly.

In becoming a plastic fanatic, you may be deluding yourself about the actual cost of something, or deferring the pain of payment until another day. But delaying the pain doesn't make it go away, it only makes it worse.

So what is the remedy? To ease yourself away from plastic dependency, here is some common-sense advice:

- Try leaving your card(s) at home when you go shopping, and pay with cash instead. For those of you who rely on your cards as a security blanket, this idea might scare you – and it should. After all, it's a lot more painful to hand a large stack of five-pound notes across the counter than to simply swipe your plastic and walk out the door with a new pair of sunglasses that you don't really need.

- Get rid of your extra credit cards, especially store cards – which are the easiest to obtain, easiest to abuse and come with the highest interest rates (up to 25 per cent). One card is sufficient, and three is the maximum. You simply don't need five, ten – or twenty-nine – credit cards, even if your credit is the very best. More credit lines only means more temptation, more bills to pay and more debt.

    Most retailers' cards charge outrageously high interest rates, but virtually all of them accept standard cards such as VISA or MasterCard.

    With only a few credit cards, you can more closely monitor your spending and see how quickly you are getting into debt: it's easy to ignore lots of little numbers, but it's hard to avoid one big number.

- Consider refinancing – that is switching from a high-interest card to one with a lower rate. Different credit cards come with different interest rates, and there is no sensible reason for you to be paying 18 per cent interest on your debt when you can be paying 12 per cent, or less.

  To find a better rate, call a number of banks and shop around. And remember: don't be shy about playing one institution off another; after all, that is the nature of Capitalism.

- Reduce your credit limit. Just because you are a customer who is profitable to a bank (that is, they earn lots of interest off your unpaid balance), doesn't mean you have to accept a bank's increase in your credit limit. If an offer to increase your limit comes through the mail, do what Nancy Reagan advised (in slightly different circumstances), and just say 'No'.

  You might even want to call your credit card's service number and lower your credit limit to a level that is sensible for you. A shocking idea, I know, but it's a way for you to exercise control and self-restraint in your spending – which can ultimately enhance your self-esteem.

- If all else fails, the final step in weaning yourself from the plastic habit is to literally cut up your cards and throw them away, like I did. If you know you are weak, then why keep the temptation at your fingertips?

  If you are guilty of charging more of your chocolate, coffee and Chinese food on your credit card than you should, then freeze them in a block of ice, or, better yet, use a blow-torch to melt them into a harmless puddle of goop – while singing after me (to the tune of 'Disco Inferno'): *'Burn, baby, burn, credit card inferno . . . !'*

  And when you have calmed down a bit, don't forget to write or call the issuers of the cards to cancel your accounts.

One final note: you may want to consolidate all of your out-standing debt on to one card with a low interest rate – as long as it is *only* one card, and you *promise* to use it responsibly. (Remember, when you consolidate to one card, you must cancel all your other accounts.) In today's world, you often need a credit card for emergencies, or collateral, such as when you rent a car, or to guarantee hotel rooms or pay for plane tickets. While you can pay for the car rental with cash, cheque or debit card, a credit card is often more convenient for all concerned. Other-wise, place the credit card in the back of a drawer, try to forget you have it, pay off your debt and learn to exist in a plastic-free world.

STEERING YOUR WAY TO A CAR LOAN

Car dealers make it sound so easy to buy that gleaming new dream-machine in the centre of the showroom floor: rather than talk about the huge dollop of cash a new car will cost you (it may be as much as you earn annually), the dealer convinces you to buy on credit, with 'manageable monthly payments'.

You think to yourself: *that doesn't sound so bad. In fact, it's cheap. I guess this chap really has my best interests at heart.* Well, guess again.

What the dealer hasn't bothered to mention is that the loan comes with a significant interest rate, that you will be paying every month, for *years.* Plus, car loans are notoriously difficult to refinance. That means you'll be stuck with a high rate indefinitely, no matter what happens to interest rates in general.

As usual, there are insurance and registration fees, and main-tenance and repair costs, to figure into your total expenditure. And don't forget that a new car starts to depreciate (its resale value drops) the minute you drive it out of the showroom.

Tip:

- If you plan to buy a car on credit, check with a few banks first to get an idea of their current car loan rates. Then, once you find the right set of wheels, get the dealer to commit to an exact price before you discuss his financing arrangements. This way, you go into a major purchase with your eyes wide open.

So you should shop for a car conservatively, and ask yourself: is this purchase really necessary? Can I afford the debt, or am I better off buying a decent used car and paying for it with cash?

OTHER LOANS YOU CANNOT IGNORE

Student loans

Contrary to the popular view, these loans *are* a part of your personal debt, and need to be managed as such. Although student loans charge a lower interest rate than, say, car loans, they can still be a significant burden over time and you cannot afford to lose sight of them.

After you've paid off any high-rate consumer debt, you might consider paying back your student loan faster than you are required to. If you double your monthly payments, for example, you will save significant amounts of interest over time. (But remember, this scheme only makes sense if the interest rates on your loans are higher than the rates you can earn on saving or investing your money.)

Vacations and weddings

When you're baking on the beach in Mallorca, clinking champagne flutes in the City of Light, or schussing down the piste in

Gstaad, it's easy to forget about the money you're spending. And when you return from your holiday or honeymoon, the last thing your sunburned and love-addled brain wants to think about is paying bills. But you ignore them at your own peril.

Quite often, travel is underwritten almost entirely with high-interest credit. I ask people: do you want to come back from Bali with black sand in your shoes. . . and in debt? Do you want to come back from trekking the Himalayas feeling enlightened . . . and in debt? The honest answer is usually no.

The Enjoy Now, Pay Later Syndrome must reach its zenith with weddings – after all, you can justify almost any expense for your special day. Again, I ask couples: do you want to start out your new life together with flushed cheeks, a sparkling gold band on your finger . . . and a looming cloud of debt?

These are events for which it is better to plan far in advance and save for. Some moments are happier if there are no negative financial consequences.

Many people feel entitled to a holiday, regardless of the cost. It doesn't matter whether you spend your free time in Brighton or in Spain. What does matter is that you can afford to pay for it in the *short term*, and that it does not affect your other, more important personal finances.

Home equity loans (remortgaging your home)

If you own your home, you can usually borrow some 80 per cent of its value, minus the balance due on your mortgage, from a bank. Many people use home equity loans to pay for improvements around the house. The downside of such a loan is that it is essentially a second mortgage, and as a result you will have two payments to make every month. Indeed, borrowers can lose their homes if they don't repay their debt, which is a stiff penalty for new wallpaper.

Others use a second mortgage to pay off other debts, such as high-interest credit card debt. But here too there is risk. After paying off their debt, some people view their newfound freedom as a licence to rack up even more debt. This is a gross emotional and financial blunder. It reflects that the serial debtors haven't learned from their first mistake, and shows that they don't understand what they are doing to themselves, or their families, by increasing the debt load.

While Sisyphus was condemned to roll a boulder to the top of a hill only to have it roll down again, people who are chronically in debt are pushing a boulder of debt of their own making up an avoidable hill; and with every push, their debt gets bigger and heavier.

Loans from friends and family

It's tempting to borrow from those who know you best, and often it seems to make sense – especially if you are striving to pay off high-interest-rate debt. But this is a risky proposition. Money borrowed from friends and family comes with high emotional interest, which can take a lot longer to pay off than credit card interest.

Many people view their friends and family as a lender of first resort, when in fact, they should be the very last resort. If any debt *has* to be paid off, this is it, and as the borrower you are responsible. You must keep your lenders informed about what you are doing. Don't assume that because you haven't talked about it the debt has been forgiven. Remember, there is no statute of limitations on the guilt, shame and bad feelings that will result if you don't repay the loan on time. In some cases, such an emotional debt can never be fully repaid.

Although this sounds horribly formal among family and friends, it's best to write up an agreement listing the exact terms of your loan – the interest rate you will pay, for example, and the date each payment is due, and to whom the payment should be sent.

IF YOU'RE ALREADY IN DEBT, DON'T PANIC

How do you dig your way out of debt? The bad news is there is no magical answer. Most of the solution is within you, the person who created the debt. The good news is that, with discipline, there are a few basic steps you can take to start chipping away at it.

When I was deeply in debt on my twenty-nine credit cards, I couldn't bear to read my bills. It was simply too depressing. One day while I was taking a long walk and avoiding my financial problems, I remembered a lesson I had learned while weeding my family's large field of vegetables in Florida. My grandmother used to say, 'You can't think about the whole field at once. Take it row by row.' She was right; the hoeing went easier that way. Every day I'd hoe three rows; by the time I reached the end of the field, it was time to start over again from the beginning.

It was a valuable lesson that I later applied to my vast field of loans. I tried not to be overwhelmed by the cumulative debt I had incurred, but rather approached it 'row by row'. By consolidating my debt, negotiating extra grace periods, getting rid of almost all my credit cards and paying off my debt one piece at a time, I eventually eradicated all of my 'weeds'. What a relief! Having learned my lesson the hard way, I have remained largely debt-free ever since.

How does this lesson apply to you? First of all, time is on your side. You can call up your creditors and negotiate an improvement in your payment schedule. But you must adhere to the new schedule; if you miss payments, the consequences are dire. The creditors will, justifiably, become much more aggressive.

When I was negotiating my debt, I found a second job as a clerk in a department store; it was a weekend job, and every pay cheque went straight to the credit card companies. I was very disciplined about my repayment schedule, because I had no choice. I didn't like working on weekends, of course, but I thought of those extra work days as hoeing that row in our fields. I took it one day at a time, and eventually I was finished with the job.

Second, you may have some money saved that you have not considered accessible. If you have a savings account, you should consider using at least some of that money to pay off your high-interest credit card debt (although you should always leave yourself an emergency cushion in the savings account).

If you are in debt and have no savings to fall back on, then your recovery is obviously going to be more of a challenge – although it is by no means impossible. As mentioned above, you should get rid of your credit cards, apply for a debit card and perhaps even consider filing for personal bankruptcy.

CREDIT REPORTS

You may not be aware of the fact that there are companies whose entire *raison d'être* is to compile information about how you use money. These 'credit reporting agencies' – Equifax and Experian – list everything that is reported to them by bank cards, credit cards, store cards and loan sources. Their credit reports include your payment history, and whether you've ever had any major financial problems.

When you apply for a loan or credit card, lenders usually request a copy of this report from one of the major agencies to assess you as a risk. You, too, are entitled to a copy of your own credit report, for a nominal fee.

If you are applying for a major loan, it is important for you to check your credit report thoroughly first. If you are turned down for credit, the lender must provide you with a specific explanation as to why. Furthermore, you needn't passively accept what the lender says. If you have a black mark in your credit record, you *can* correct it.

Debtors' Golden Rules

National Debtline (0808 808 4000) is a national, confidential telephone helpline for people in the UK with debt problems. They suggest following these basic rules:

- Don't ignore the problem: it won't go away and the longer you leave it, the worse it gets.
- Don't borrow money to pay off your debts without thinking carefully. Get advice first. This kind of borrowing could lead to you losing your home.
- If you have lost your job, or are off work because of illness, check whether your payments are covered by payment protection insurance. Check you are claiming all the benefits you can.
- Work out your personal budget. Make sure you show it or send it to your creditors when you tell them about your difficulties.
- Get in touch with your creditors straight away and explain your difficulties. Go and see them, or phone or write to them.
- Make sure you tackle your priority debts first – for example, debts which could mean losing your home or having your gas or electricity cut off.
- Work out a reasonable offer to repay the money owed. Don't worry if it appears very small if that is really all you can afford. Creditors prefer you to pay a small amount regularly than make an offer you can't afford.
- Contact everyone you owe money to. If you make arrangements to pay some creditors but not others, you could run into difficulties again.
- If the first person you speak to is unhelpful, ask to speak to somebody more senior who may be able to agree to what you want.

- Don't give up trying to reach an agreement even if creditors are difficult.
- Fill in the reply forms to court papers and let the court have all the facts. This information will be used to decide if you owe the money and what instalments you should pay.
- Always attend court hearings. Take a copy of your personal budget with you. Don't think that going to the County Court makes you a criminal; it's not that kind of court. They will not send you to prison and there is no jury.
- Always keep copies of any letters or court forms you send or receive.

Credit reporting agencies do make mistakes from time to time. If you discover such an error, contact the agency right away and have it corrected. If there is a legitimate reason for the black mark – such as a period of illness that kept you from working for a time – then write a letter to the companies involved (with proof), seeking a resolution to your bad credit. If you achieve resolution, both you and the lending company in question (the issuer of credit, such as a credit card company, a department store or a petrol company) must write to the reporting credit agency requesting that your information is updated. By doing this, you will effectively correct your bad credit report.

If, however, you do not reach a resolution, you can still send a letter to the reporting agency, giving your side of events; this letter will be kept in your file. But your black mark will stand, meaning it will be more difficult for you to obtain credit of any kind, be it a home mortgage, a car loan or even a student loan.

Learning how to use debt properly is tricky. Some people will always abuse debt, no matter what the consequences; but for the vast majority of us, all we need is a basic understanding of how debt works, an insight into our own financial strengths and weaknesses, a desire to correct our mistakes and a commitment to avoid long-term, high-interest debt.

CHAPTER 4

SAVE YOURSELF:
THE ART AND SCIENCE OF SAVING

The Alvin Hall Quick Quiz on Saving

Are you a Sensible Saver or a Psycho Spender?

- Does the possibility of accumulating money excite you?
- Have you set yourself an annual savings target and do you stick to it?
- Do you save enough so that you feel just a little squeezed every month?
- Do you keep the money in your savings account sacred, and use only your current account for living expenses?
- Do you have 3–6 months of your income in a savings account?
- Do you put money in your savings account before you buy those 'little treats' each month?

If you answered 'No' to any of these questions, then you need to learn to save more and spend less, starting right now.

When people meet me, they often assume that I have always been part of the comfortable socio-economic stratum that I inhabit in New York City. But the truth is I grew up in rural Wakulla County, Florida, in circumstances that were almost the complete opposite of my life today.

More than a hand-to-mouth existence, it was a make-do life; whatever you had on your plate was *all* you had, and the hope for more didn't exist. There were nine of us in a modest house – seven kids, my mother and my grandmother. We had no insurance. We survived with the help of Welfare. We worked a tired plot of land to raise okra, green beans, corn, new potatoes, tomatoes, snap beans and sugar peas. We had little cash income, and I took my first paying job, aged thirteen, as a dishwasher, at the Aloha Restaurant in a town called (ironically) Panacea. So, when people say that they have 'no money left at the end of the week' to put into their savings account, I know exactly what they mean.

Yet, somehow, my grandmother, Rosa Lee Hall, managed to squirrel away little bits of money here and there. Unbeknownst to the rest of us, she gradually managed to save $20,000 (£12,000) this way – a tremendous amount, under the circumstances – which she carefully hid in a place that was close to her heart: neatly tucked inside her bra cups!

I tell this story because I know that in even the worst circumstances it's possible to save some money. While my grandmother managed to keep her treasure safe, I do not recommend her methods. Better to put your hard-earned money in a more conventional place, such as a building society or money market fund, where it will safely earn you interest. And remember, as my grandmother liked to say, 'Every little bit takes you a step closer towards a better life.'

HOW TO SUCCEED IN SAVING

Oikonomos, the Greek root of the English word 'economy', translates to 'household manager'. And, in a sense, the science of economics is not really so different from the art of wisely managing everyday household expenses.

The traditional housewife was given a fixed budget and had little choice but to stick to it rigidly. She was constantly monitoring the cost of everyday life – from the price of oranges to that of shampoo, and even the price of her husband's socks. These housewives were generally practical, could make do on limited resources and intuitively knew good value when they saw it.

But now, at the end of the twentieth century, times are changing. With more people joining the workforce, a high divorce rate and an increase in freelance work – combined with a culture of easy credit and rampant consumerism – the priorities and economics of our society are shifting. Our priorities are now speed and convenience, while thriftiness and economy have become less important in our day-to-day lives. We work longer hours than our parents did, so we feel we don't have time to shop, look for bargains and cook wonderful meals at home. Roles that were traditionally filled by mothers and housewives are being replaced by service businesses, such as cleaners, restaurants and daycare centres.

Yes, that poached salmon with herbed dill sauce costs 25 to 30 per cent more at the take-away, but it's easy to buy, delicious to eat and it's yours to take home without a second thought.

Indeed, many successful business people are efficient at the office but less practical when it comes to their personal finances. They seem keen to make money but are reluctant to manage it, or even to talk about it. In such an environment, people are losing sight of the importance of saving.

One such friend, a fashion designer I'll call Ellen, organised a brilliant pension scheme for herself through her job. Once she had done that, though, she assumed that she had taken care of her personal finances for ever. Caught up in her glamorous, fast-paced life, she failed to monitor her other personal expenses, although she always made the required contributions to her pension.

The result? One day she realised, with a shock, that she had been spending a huge amount of her take-home pay, and was carrying an ever-increasing amount of credit card debt.

What did she do? Nothing. Ellen didn't want to change her lifestyle. In fact, she felt she deserved to play hard because she worked so hard. She ignored the problem, and hoped that it would resolve itself. It didn't, of course; it only grew worse. Finally, when her personal debt grew so onerous that the practical side of her brain told her she could no longer ignore it, she called me, hoping I would help her sort it out.

What I thought was, 'Sinner, heal thyself!', but I would never say that. In the end, I gave Ellen the practical advice that is my own mantra: 'Saving is a necessity, not a luxury.'

For most of us, putting aside a fixed amount of perfectly good money each month is hard work, but the fact is you *can* save, even if it's only a small amount. No matter what your age, gender, race or professional status, you should think of saving as *a fixed monthly expense*, a regular part of your budget, just like your car or mortgage payments. As a rule, you should aim to save at least 5 to 10 per cent of your pay each month.

*   *   *

Six Simple Saving Schemes

1 Think of saving as a fixed monthly expense. Saving is something you *must* do, like paying your mortgage, even if it's only a small amount every month.

   While there is no magical number for how much you should save, 10 per cent of your monthly income is a realistic amount to aim for. If you manage to save more than that, all the better. Some financial professionals recommend that you put 10 per cent a month into your retirement scheme alone, and another 5 per cent into a savings account.

2 Use the money in your current account to pay your daily living expenses, and keep the money in your savings account sacrosanct. You should aim to build up a cushion of no less than three months' income in your savings account, for emergencies.

3 To make saving easier, enroll in a savings plan that automatically deducts money (the amount is determined by you) from your current account each month. That way, you won't be tempted to spend it.

4 Don't save your hard-earned money under the mattress, where a mouse or a burglar might find it; instead, invest in a pension scheme such as the state-sponsored Individual Savings Accounts (ISA – see page 159). Inaugurated in April 1999 (they replace TESSAs and PEPs), ISAs allow you to put money away for the future on a tax-free basis.

5 Invest in a money market fund. Nearly as safe as a bank's saving account, these funds pay a higher interest rate. You can buy a money market fund through a unit trust company, a brokerage firm or a bank. And you can have money automatically drawn from your pay cheque and placed in the fund before you get your hands on it.

6 Set a savings target for the year – 10 per cent of your annual income, at a minimum – to give yourself something to aim for. If you reach your goal early, treat yourself. Spend the equivalent of what you put away each month – new (not saved) money – on something you really want; it's a treat that you have earned. If you don't achieve your goal early, bear down and keep saving until you do. Then celebrate!

Saving did not come naturally to me. But when I had to borrow money in order to move for a new job, I began to think about other unexpected costs: what if I had been faced with a medical emergency, or a car that wouldn't start, or a house fire, then what would I have done? It was then that I began to understand the importance of saving for the future.

At first, I thought, 'I don't know where to begin.' But then, as in the inspirational refrain from the musical *A Chorus Line*, I said to myself: 'I can do that!'

Saving a portion of the money I earned, I realised, was like paying myself for the work I was doing. To get started, I turned saving into a game: I set myself monthly, then annual saving targets. The better I got at saving, the higher I'd raise the bar. If I hit my target on or before schedule, I'd buy myself a treat such as a dinner out.

As I became more sophisticated about the ways in which to save, I'd tell myself, 'You're not saving hard enough unless it hurts just a bit.'

Today, saving has become such a regular habit for me that I hardly think twice about it; it's like learning to ride a bike – once you know how to save you don't forget it. As a result, I have stored up a year's worth of earnings in a high-interest bank account.

Why save so much? The amount of savings you keep is a

matter of finding your own comfort level. In my case, there are some pretty obvious psychological reasons for why financial security is important. I was raised with little money, I've seen tragedy and know it can strike unexpectedly, I work freelance and am therefore more vulnerable should I lose my work, and I've had to confront prejudice in the business world.

While this last factor may not be something you have had to deal with, you probably have issues of your own to confront. Maybe you are poor, or a single woman, or are getting on in years, or are so young that others don't take you seriously. The fact of the matter is that today almost *everyone* needs to guard their financial future carefully. Indeed, more people than ever are freelancing; rapid technological change and the global marketplace are destroying millions of traditional jobs and creating millions of new ones; companies are constantly merging, reorganising, and downsizing; and changes in the government social policies are fraying the old safety nets. Even if you have a job in a large firm, you can't afford to assume that you have lifetime security. You owe it to yourself to make your own provisions for an uncertain future.

Best of all, the money you save is *all yours.* Your savings will insulate you from some of life's nasty surprises, and give you greater control over your own destiny. In a sense, it buys you mental and physical freedom. Once people really understand what that means, it can be a very powerful motivator. It is for me.

Why do I put a year's worth of income in a savings account that pays a low interest rate? The money I have saved at the bank is not earning as much interest as it would if it were in the stock market, of course, but it is also not subject to the risks of the market. In a savings account your money is *risk-free.* The knowledge that my savings are safe and sound, and instantly available should I need them, gives me peace of mind and lets me sleep at night.

TRUE-LIFE SAVING STORIES

Some of the richest people in the world are among the most conservative when it comes to their own savings. Like me, they like the security of knowing they are always prepared, no matter what.

These true-life savings stories should provide food for thought:

- Sherry Lansing, a one-time teacher and actress, made headlines for being the first woman to run a Hollywood movie studio – a notoriously expensive and risky business. As Chairman and CEO of the Paramount Motion Picture Group, she has gambled and won on such mega-hits as *Titanic*, *Saving Private Ryan* and *The Truman Show* – and has earned millions of dollars doing so. So where does this tough, risk-taking woman put her own hard-won cash? Reportedly, she invests much of it in super-safe US government securities.

- Joel, a friend of mine who is a very successful Wall Street wheeler-dealer, works with the stock market every day. So where does this financially sophisticated man keep his money? He keeps all of his fortune in a 'very boring, very conservative' money-market account. Why? He has a family that he wants to protect. While his career depends on the unnerving ups and downs of the stock market, he doesn't want the same volatility for his savings.

- Another friend who had a large divorce settlement, also put her money in US government securities, one of the safest investments in the world. Emma didn't invest in the stock market, she says, because her government securities give her 'plenty to live on, and they are totally safe. Why do I need to take unnecessary risks to make more money?'

THE MONEY DIET: YOU CAN NEVER BE TOO RICH OR TOO THIN

Here are a few common-sense savings strategies to help keep your finances fit.

Put yourself on a savings regimen

'Little strokes fell great oaks,' Benjamin Franklin lectured, and the lesson applies equally to saving money. You can put away an amazing amount if you do it habitually, a little at a time.

Making savings a habit is like having a healthy exercise regimen. Everyone's physical tolerances are different and so are our tolerances for saving, but the key is consistency: save regularly and save often. Set yourself a savings target – say 5 to 10 per cent of your income every month. Then make a standing order for that amount to go out of your current account and into a savings account the day after you are paid. (Any bank can make the arrangements for you.) Tell yourself that those savings are sacrosanct, and make sure you don't dip into them for some mad fling.

If you have a problem with self-discipline, put the money into an account that only allows you to make a few withdrawals every year. And don't forget to keep an eye on your interest rate, which will change over time.

Part of maintaining your savings regimen is to monitor your accounts at least once a quarter. Take a look at your statements, and make sure that the correct interest is being credited to you: banks, after all, aren't always perfect. Also, check to see if your bank has another type of savings account or time deposit available, which pays a higher interest than you are currently earning; if so, find out if you can shift your money into it without paying a penalty.

Believe it or not: saving can be fun

We all like treats, and when I was learning to save I used a carrot-and-stick approach with myself to make it less of a chore. For example, if your goal is to save £3,000 in a year, and you achieve that goal by September, then reward yourself with a treat – spend £200 (of new, not saved money) on something you really want, like a swish piece of clothing from Gucci, or tickets to a favourite sports match. You deserve a treat because you set your goal, stuck to it and accomplished it ahead of schedule.

Plan your pension

When you reach the point that you need to replace your Boxercise workouts with *t'ai chi*, you'll need to have some money in a retirement account to cover your expenses. At today's interest rates you'd need to have some £350,000 in your pension fund to give yourself an annual income of £15,000 a year, after retirement, for the rest of your life.

Be prepared

If you are single you need to be prepared to handle life's unexpected lurches on your own. If you lose your job, or become so sick that you cannot earn, how are you going to pay your monthly bills?

If you are a woman, you need to be particularly careful about saving because you may find there are times when you're not earning much – if at all – because you may be looking after children or relatives. There is nothing wrong with doing those things; in fact they are often essential. But with your changed status you are still spending, and not putting money in the bank. What happens to preparing for your own future?

Save your savings

One reason to save money is to protect yourself. But how do you protect what you've saved? It's worth investigating the different types of insurance that are designed to protect your finances should things go wrong. There are many kinds of insurance – including redundancy, critical illness, permanent health, payment protection, and so on. The list is endless; don't buy them all; shop around, ask for advice and choose the plan that suits you best.

One way to winnow your choices is to think about the problems that would hurt your finances most, and insure yourself against them. (See Chapter 8, where insurance is explained in greater detail.)

The Power of Compounding Interest

Compounding – earning interest on the interest generated by your account – is a powerful, if often overlooked, tool to grow your money.

If in 1980 you had started to regularly save £100 per month in a typical bank's Instant Access Account, and you have reinvested all the interest in the account, your money would have compounded like this:

Time period	£100/month	Value of account
Oct 1980–Oct 1990	£12,000	£16,143.51
Oct 1980–Oct 2000	£24,000	£48,540.72

(Source: Nationwide)

As this chart shows, the longer you continue to regularly invest, the faster your money piles up. As a friend of mine says, 'Compounding is like the wind under the wings of a jet. The plane starts down the runway slowly, but as it picks up speed the wind lifts its wings and it takes off.' Similarly, compounding will raise the value of your account faster and faster over time.

The magic of compounding

One of the most important, and least understood, benefits of saving is the effect of 'compounding', which is when you earn interest on your interest.

Here's how compounding works: if you have £1,000 in a savings account that earns 6 per cent interest per annum, you will have earned £60 by the end of one year, leaving you a total balance of £1,060. The next year you will earn 6 per cent on £1060, or £63.60, for a total balance of £1,123.60. By the third year, you will have earned £67.42 in interest, for a total of £1,191.02 (assuming your interest rate remains steady at 6 per cent).

Every year, then, you are earning interest on your previous year's interest. Thus, the longer your money remains in the account, the faster it grows – until, after a few years, the pace of the increase can be amazing.

In this example, the 6 per cent interest is credited annually, but in the real world it can be credited to your account monthly, or even daily. Hence, the effects of compounding result in your money growing faster.

THE PROBLEM WITH PARSIMONIOUSNESS

Believe it or not, there are cases when too *much* saving can be a bad thing. I know people who have saved and saved, at the expense of almost everything else, and the result is they have turned into mean curmudgeons – like the living descendants of certain Dickens' characters. These are examples you should try not to emulate:

- An acquaintance in Manhattan whom I'll call Angela is constantly poor-mouthing: she won't eat at nice restaurants because they are 'too expensive'; refuses to go to

Broadway plays because 'they shouldn't cost so much'; and buys the cheap copies of expensive perfumes because, she says, 'Who needs to pay all that money to smell good?' One day Angela invited me to her flat, and I was surprised at how grand and opulent it was. It turned out she comes from a very well-to-do family, and can easily afford the very best in life.

To her credit, Angela has not squandered her inheritance. But her fixation on frugality has warped her perspective on what constitutes healthy saving. A lovely woman, over time she became pinched and neurotic about money. She is in the autumn of life now, and she should treat herself to something she loves once in a while, while she still can.

- Another case is a man I know who comes from a lower-middle-class family, who has become a successful solicitor and earns a very good salary. But somehow he has never learned to enjoy life. Paul saves a percentage of his income that is greater than the average person spends in a year. In fact, the accumulation of money seems to be the main focus of his life. But, sadly, he has never learned to be generous with himself, or with his friends.

When we go out to dinner together, for example, Paul always demands that we each pay for what we eat, exactly. His portion, of course, is always the smaller – a fact he loves to point out. Although he earns a very good salary, he has never once offered to pick up the tab. Indeed, the more money he makes, the worse Paul's miserliness gets. And that is one reason why we haven't had a meal together in a very long time.

THE ALVIN HALL LAW OF SEX

The common thread in the above examples is a lack of *generosity*. What, you may ask, does generosity have to do with saving?

The *Alvin Hall Law of Sex* states: 'It's not about technique, it's about generosity.' And you could say the same holds true of money management, or, indeed, life in general. Success in bed comes from a mutual give and take; but if you are in bed with someone who is not generous, you might begin to wonder whether you'd have more fun all alone. Good sex, as with good saving, is all about balance.

To really enjoy life we must learn how to give as well as to take. People who accumulate money and use it sensibly, both for saving and spending, are able to maintain a healthy balance in life.

The key to successful saving is to set yourself rules and stick to them, but not to become obsessed with hoarding money. Or, as my friend Ted says, 'It's about eating *one* doughnut, enjoying it and not gobbling up all the extra doughnuts.'

Spending and Saving Excuses

In the course of my researches around the UK, I have heard many of the same stories about why people can't be bothered to learn about personal finance responsibility. Indeed, I've heard these stories so many times that I have begun to keep a list of some of the more pernicious money myths that people cling to:

- *The Myth of False Optimism*
  Some people choose to ignore their personal finances because they believe that as long as they have enough in the till to cover their expenses today, they'll be OK tomorrow. I call this 'false optimism', or 'wilful ignorance', and I ask its practitioners: what would happen if your pay-cheque didn't arrive on time, or you got sick or injured, or you suddenly lost your job?

  The answer, of course, is that the False Optimist has no reserves in place, no real idea of what he or she will do next, and faces a bleak future on the dole.

- *The Ostrich Myth*
  Others say they would really like to have more control over their personal finances, but feel overwhelmed by the vast amount of choices and information available. They become frozen, intimidated or distracted, and in the end do nothing. I think of these people as 'Ostriches' because they are virtually sticking their heads in the sand and hoping, like Candide, for the best of all possible worlds.

  Unfortunately, reality tends to be messy and unpredictable and I'm afraid the Ostrich is no better prepared for life's vicissitudes than the False Optimist. In either case, a lack of knowledge and action means that a person is not in good financial health.

- *The Nanny Myth*
  The stubborn belief that someone, or something – lottery winnings, a family inheritance, your employer, the government, your beloved childhood nanny – will take care of your financial needs for ever. Don't count on it. Educate yourself, and start saving and investing right now.

- *The Prince Charming/Toy Boy Myth*
  The belief that a sexy, rich, honest Ms or Mr Right is about to appear around the corner, pick you up in her/his Ferrari and spirit you away to a life of glamorous leisure at her/his Monte Carlo palazzo.

  Well, maybe it will happen that way. But until it does, you'd better get a handle on your credit-card addiction, your mobile phone bills and your penchant for pricey Belgian chocolates and learn how to take care of yourself.

  Even if the ugly toad you met in the caf turns out to be Lord Dreamcometrue when you kiss him, there is always a chance that your match-made-in-Hollywood won't last for ever. If that happens, then you will find yourself on the street, older and less employable. This will make it difficult to survive in the manner to which you have become accustomed.

- *The Spring Chicken Myth*
  The belief that if you are young and foot-loose, you have plenty of time to get serious about boring old things such as savings accounts, pension plans and paying credit card bills on time. Guess what? You're wrong!

  Time flies when you're having fun. But before you know it, you'll be an adult, which comes with certain (financial) responsibilities. If you save nothing, and rack up a huge credit card debt now, you will be paying it off for years to come – at a grinding rate of interest. Which means that flower garden or Aston Martin you've always dreamed of will remain just that, a dream.

In truth, you need to start thinking about your finances straight out of university. Learn to save, invest and – yes – spend, responsibly.

- *The Lion in Winter Myth*
Also known as the 'It's Too Late to Change' myth. Those fatalists who believe they are too old or stuck in their ways to learn new tricks, like how to save for retirement, are just as self-deluding as those who believe they are too young to learn about balancing income versus spending.

  If you start saving now, no matter how old you are, it can only have a positive impact on your overall financial health.

- *The 'Smart Investor' Myth*
Those speculators who are always on the prowl for a 'guaranteed' quick killing are doomed to disappointment. The men and women who constantly try to beat the odds, hit the right lottery number, parlay every stock tip from the local barman into a fantastic investment, are missing the point.

  Truly smart investing is not about making millions overnight. It's about diligent research, making informed choices and managing your investments for steady growth over the long term. It may not be as thrilling as gambling all your pension money in one wild night in Las Vegas, but it's less stressful and the pay-off is better than a losing number on the roulette wheel.

- *The 'Expert' Myth*
The belief that only those who possess a PhD in High Finance can understand how to save and invest money

- wisely. This myth is nurtured (deliberately, in some cases) by those authors, commentators and financial whizzkids who stand to profit from everyone else's fear and ignorance. They enjoy using exclusionary language and high-falutin' concepts to intimidate lowly citizens, but this often means they don't believe, or understand, what they are saying themselves.

  The Expert Myth is disproven every day by amateur investors from every walk of life who routinely equal or out-perform the City professionals.

- *The 'Rich Don't Do It, Why Should I?' Myth*
  Many Britons depend on the advice of financial advisers. While this is not necessarily a bad thing, provided the advice is good, I tell people to educate themselves about their own finances as much as possible, and to rely on the professionals only when necessary – and with their eyes wide open.

  There is a widely-held belief that when the rich hire a financial professional, they automatically abdicate any and all responsibility for how their money is managed. This is absurd. All of the wealthy people I know want to stay that way, even those who give a lot of time and money away to charity, and they are deeply involved in managing their money along *with* their financial advisers. After all, the more you know, the more informed your choices are and the more you can get out of your adviser. It's your money, and your life; wouldn't you like to have a say in how it's managed? (For more on financial advisers, please see Chapter 9.)

- *The Myths of Debt*
  Some believe that life is meant to be lived in a state of perpetual debt, while others are convinced that any

amount of debt, no matter how small or short-lived, is evil incarnate. Both assumptions are wrong.

You will never pay off your credit card debt if you keep charging new purchases on your cards and pay only the minimum monthly payment.

And yet, if you pay your bill every month, credit cards offer a way of buying things with what really amounts to a short-term, interest-free loan.

CHAPTER 5

HEARTH AND HOME

The Alvin Hall Quick Quiz on Buying Property

When you think about buying a house, it's easier to fantasise about what kind of cabinets you'd like to have in the kitchen, the type of wallpaper you'd like in the hallway, or the colour you'll paint the lounge, than to focus on what sort of mortgage you'll need, and how you'll afford it five years hence. You needn't give up blue-sky dreaming, but make time for some down-to-earth planning as well.

Here's a quick property reality check:

- Do you recognise the inherent risk in buying property for investment?
- Have you investigated whether you'd be better off buying than renting your home?
- Do you know the difference between an endowment mortgage and a repayment mortgage?
- Did you read the fine print on your mortgage agreement?
- Do you know the interest rate you're paying on your mortgage?
- Have you set a budget for your home improvements?

If you answered 'No' to any of these questions, then you'll need to pay special attention to the following chapter.

Purchasing property can be one of the most rewarding experiences in life, in every sense, but it can also be one of the most time-consuming, financially draining and emotionally unsettling aspects of managing your personal finances.

Whether you are buying a property to live in or to let, everyone wants to believe that they will make money on it. After all, a house looks like a solid investment, it seems that it will always be in demand and there are plenty of people who have hit the jackpot by buying property. But the truth is there is no guarantee that you will make a profit on your property, or even recoup your investment.

A house is not simply another investment: it is generally the largest expenditure you'll ever make; it comes with all sorts of financial and emotional strings attached; and since you will probably live in it, anything that makes it seem less than ideal goes right to your emotions. In short, the decision to buy a place should not be undertaken lightly – as the following true cautionary tale should make clear.

During a period when property values were hot, my friend Louise decided to buy a house because she didn't want to 'keep throwing her money away on rent', and because she was 'afraid of missing the market'. The house she bought was a charming but quirky place, situated on a busy street and near enough to the tube that you could feel a gentle rumble every time a train passed by. She loved her new home and spent lots of money and time decorating it to suit her own taste.

After five years, though, Louise decided that she'd like a larger house with more of a garden. The property market, in the meantime, had remained flat. When she put her house up for sale, my friend discovered there were very few takers. Louise was shocked: after all, it was a charming place and she had devoted a lot of energy to making it beautiful. When she tried to let it, she discovered that she would not even cover the cost of her mortgage. Months later, when the house was finally sold, it went for less than what she had paid for it. Louise never even recouped one penny of the money she'd spent on decorating. With less money than she had anticipated for a new place, she moved to an even smaller house, albeit in a better location.

First-time homebuyers, particularly, need to remember that while many people have made money on property, most have done so over the long term, and there are no guarantees.

TO RENT OR TO BUY – THAT SHOULD BE THE FIRST QUESTION

Why do you want to buy a property? Perhaps you are fed up with sharing your space with flatmates, your landlord doesn't keep the building clean, or you are tired of moving from one rented place to another. Maybe you're feeling pressurised to buy a place because you hear from friends and relatives that interest rates are low and house prices are rising. Maybe you'd like the financial security and rewards that seem to come with owning a home. Or maybe you are simply feeling that now is the time in life to buy a place of your own.

These are all valid reasons for wanting to buy a home. But the British are obsessed with the idea that it is always better to buy a property than to rent – 'renting is a waste of money' is the catchphrase you hear parroted over and over again – but this is not necessarily true, especially if you are young. I realise this is a nearly heretical notion; but I have thought a lot about this in my own life and would caution you to think very carefully about whether it really makes sense for you to buy at this point in your life.

The purchase of a home is frequently the most significant investment people make in the course of their lives. Yet, because of the emotions associated with 'home', it is difficult for people to think about this enormous expenditure as rationally as they do about investments in, say, stocks or bonds. In buying property you are not only locking up a significant amount of money in your deposit, but you are tethering yourself to the place and to big monthly mortgage payments for years to come. Despite the stories you hear about people striking gold in property resales, the truth is there are no guarantees that you will recoup your investment – let alone make a profit.

If you rent, on the other hand, you can use that large chunk of deposit money in other ways. You are free to simply pick up and go for an extended trip, for example, or to invest your money in securities – which will probably give you a better return than property in the long run.

Indeed, it was this line of thinking that guided my decision to rent a flat for the first thirteen years I lived in New York City. My decision was totally numbers-based. When I first moved to the Big Apple in the mid-1980s, almost every person I met was scrambling to buy a place; the market was super-heated, and owning was simply 'the thing to do'. By scraping together all I had, I could afford a modest deposit and was tempted to buy. But in a moment of clarity, I sat down and crunched the numbers, and realised that it simply didn't make sense. Instead, I rented a decent flat, travelled to places I had always dreamed about – Egypt, Peru, Tierra del Feugo, Russia – and invested some of my money in the stock market. It happened that I hit an 'up' market, and my investments grew nicely. By the time the worldwide recession hit the New York property market in the early 1990s, I had made and saved enough to buy a much larger apartment than I could have afforded a decade or so earlier. At that point the scales had tipped in the other direction; the numbers indicated that it *did* make sense for me to buy, and so I did.

The case for renting

As someone who rents, you have fewer responsibilities and more flexibility than you do as an owner. You can enjoy your free time instead of worrying about maintenance costs; if you want to move, you can do so much more quickly and easily than if you have to sell; and, rather than tie up a huge chunk of your money in a house, you can invest it.

After a bit of research, you may conclude that it makes better sense for you to invest your savings in liquid assets – such as stocks, bonds or unit trusts – than property. Liquid assets will make your money much more accessible than property, and can provide a better return.

The case for buying

In a super-heated property market, your monthly mortgage payments can be cheaper than rent, especially over the long term. If you stay in your home for a decent amount of time, you will build equity in your property; by the time you pay off your mortgage, your house will generally be worth more than you paid for it. Further, as someone who rents, your long-term costs will be subject to inflation.

Before you start visiting estate agents, however, you need to take stock of where you are in your life, and consider some of the difficult financial and emotional issues that buying property entails.

Dangerous Emotional Statements People Make About Real Estate

- I have to buy right now, before prices go any higher.
- I have to buy before interest rates go up.
- I have to buy because I've heard I can save money through the tax benefits of a mortgage.
- All my friends are buying property, I feel as if I should be buying too.

It's all in the timing

Financially, it makes sense to buy a place only if you plan on living there for at least three years, and preferably five or more years; experts say that seven years is the average length of time most people stay in their first home.

Planning to live in a house for a short period of time and then renting it out is all the rage in the UK now. While this can make sense in the long term, don't underestimate the costs and headaches of being a landlord. A house won't maintain itself, after all, and the more frequent the turnover of your tenants the higher your costs will be. Also, bear in mind that most people need to sell their first home in order to afford the next one.

Finally, be sure you have made a proper budget, triple-checked your sums, and put a finger to the wind: if buying to let is too trendy, then avoid it. According to an article in the *Financial Times*, for example, everyone seemed to alight on the idea of buying-to-let at the same time in the late 1990s. The result? Property prices in central London rose while rents fell, and all those starry-eyed investors were in for a nasty shock. Net yields in that area fell to 4.3 per cent – and were forecasted to dip below 4 per cent – compared with net yields of nearly 7 per cent at the start of the decade. As they used to say in Rome, *Caveat emptor* – 'Let the buyer beware.'

Location, location, location

Maybe you have saved enough to put down a deposit, or a relative has given you some money and you think the time is right to buy. First, take a good hard look at what kinds of homes are available, and where they are located, before you get too excited. You may not be able to afford the type of home you're looking for in the location you'd like to be in. In real estate, location is crucial.

Then, before you go house hunting, visit a bank or building society and find out how much you can afford to spend. They can walk you through a calculation based on your credit history and current income.

Prioritise

Don't kid yourself: owning a home isn't cheap. Before you take the plunge, work out how much you spend on 'fun' things, such as entertainment and holidays, and ask yourself whether you are *really* prepared to sacrifice those luxuries for the sake of owning a property.

Unmarrieds take note

Are you buying alone or together? If you are unmarried and buying a property together, remember that such a purchase is a lot more financially and legally binding than living together in a rented property.

The sad fact is that if you live together before you marry, you are statistically more likely to divorce. So if you are going to buy together you need to have a lawyer draw up a legal agreement that includes, among other things: the specific percentage of property ownership each will have, the conditions under which the property can be sold in a dispute, how one partner can buy the other out, how the monies will be disbursed when the property is sold and how a dispute will be arbitrated. This document can also factor in the savings you have each put aside for the deposit, the move and the decorating costs in determining fair ownership rights – and the distribution of the proceeds from the sale of the property.

It is best to have a lawyer draw up this agreement for you, even though it will require paying a fee (roughly £200 to £400). This up-front fee will certainly be cheaper than hiring a lawyer to help you solve any problems should the relationship turn sour.

Ideally, when buying a property together, you should each be able to afford it independently, in case you should split up. If you can't manage that, you should consider having one of you buy the home and the other pay rent, with a proper, legally binding lease which gives the renter security.

Kids cost

Children are wonderful, but they are much more expensive than you might imagine. Can you afford to own a house and have a child, or two? (See Chapter 6.)

Pensions are important

It is more important to put your money into a pension plan than to buy a house. Can you afford your mortgage payments on top of your contributions towards your pension?

DEPOSIT

The first question most home buyers ask is: what price can I afford?

The more you deposit up front, the smaller your mortgage payments will be. I'd suggest a deposit of about 20 to 30 per cent of the purchase price. If you need a mortgage for more than 80 per cent of the value of the property, you usually have to pay a higher interest rate and extra charges.

Finding enough money for a deposit is the biggest obstacle for most first-time home buyers. I know it was for me. It's not a good idea to borrow this money, because you're using a loan to take out an even bigger loan – thus piling debt on top of debt. And don't feel that by delaying you are necessarily missing a once-in-a-lifetime opportunity. The housing market tends to be cyclical, and if you wait you might just snap up a bargain. On the other hand, some lenders will give 100 per cent mortgages – especially if you are a first-time home-buyer with a good credit record – although the fees will be higher. I am very much against 100 per cent mortgages. They simply encourage people who cannot really afford to buy a home to take on enormous debt. While a 100 per cent mortgage may seem like a helping hand for those in need, don't forget that nothing comes free. Borrowing the whole purchase price of your house is a huge gamble – maybe even a gamble on your entire future. In order for a 100 per cent mortgage to work out, your property has got to steadily increase in value just to cover the costs of your moving to a new house. It is unlikely you will see a penny of profit in such a scheme. If the market falls, or you lose your job, or your neighbourhood becomes suddenly unfashionable – as with London's Docklands in the early 1990s – then you could find yourself in very deep trouble indeed. My advice is to delay buying a property until you've saved enough money for a decent deposit.

MORTGAGE BASICS

A mortgage is a loan that you use to pay for a home; it is 'secured' by your property, meaning that if you don't pay it back the lender can evict you and sell your home in order to get its money back.

How Much Home Can You Afford to Buy?

Typical lending criteria are as follows:

- A single income borrower can take up to 3.25 times their salary – i.e., a salary of £20,000 will produce a loan of £65,000.
- Joint income borrowers can take 3.25 times the higher salary plus 1 times the lower salary, or 2.5 times the joint salary – i.e., with a high salary of £20,000 and a lower salary of £15,000 the total mortgage by the first calculation could be £80,000. By the second calculation it will be £87,500.

(*Source*: Halifax)

Mortgage payments consist of *interest*, the fee you are charged by a bank, building society or mortgage company to borrow money, and/or *principal*, the amount you borrow from the lender. The average term for mortgages is twenty-five years, although the term may vary from five years to thirty years. To minimise costs, you should try to borrow as little money as possible on your mortgage, and pay it back as quickly as possible. Generally, you shouldn't spend more than 30 per cent of your take-home pay on mortgage repayments. In other words, a mortgage is a big debt – and a big responsibility.

To determine whether you qualify for a mortgage, and if so what size mortgage, lenders will look at the following:

Show me the money

Mortgage payments are the single largest monthly expense for many people. When determining how much you can afford to borrow, therefore, lenders primarily look at your annual income and how much you owe. They also look at your credit report to see how responsibly you have handled debt (credit cards, store cards, car loans) in the past. They want to be sure you can pay for your new home, after all, and that you can be trusted to pay their loan back, with interest, on time.

As a single person, you can generally borrow up to three times your annual income to purchase a home; as a married couple, you can borrow up to two and a half times your combined income. Add any money you have saved for a deposit. But these are rough estimates, and the amount of a loan often depends on interest rates. When doing your sums, don't forget that when interest rates rise, so will your monthly payment.

Debt is a don't
Lenders also look at your current debt – especially such things as student loans, car loans and credit card payments. To their minds, a lot of debt means you will have less money to put towards your housing costs. They also try to determine your future monthly housing costs and calculate what portion of your monthly income will be devoted to these expenses.

A clean credit report is a beautiful thing
To make sure you are someone who pays back loans, lenders will check the history of your financial behaviour in a credit report. If you've defaulted on a loan recently, or been late on loan or bill payments, you may have difficulty getting a bank to give you a mortgage.

On the other hand, *no* credit report can be a nightmare, too. If you've never used credit cards, or taken out a loan, and your first major purchase is a house, then mortgage lenders won't necessarily want to be the ones to find out if you are a trustworthy borrower.

Keep your job
Lenders like to see that you have worked in the same job, or the same industry, for at least two years. If you are someone who has

bounced around from place to place, they are likely to view you with suspicion; ditto for freelancers.

BUYING PROPERTY

Once you've decided that you *need* to buy a property now, and can afford it, the question is what kind of mortgage should you get?

There are so many different payment schemes available that the average consumer can be easily confused, and mortgage literature is frequently hard to decipher. Don't worry, the bottom line is that there are really only two ways to pay your loan – by a *repayment* mortgage or by an *interest-only* mortgage (one type of which is called an *endowment* mortgage). The question you need to ask yourself is: how do you want to pay your loan back – bit by bit, as with a repayment mortgage, or all in one go at the end of its term, as with an interest-only mortgage?

A Repayment mortgage

This is a very simple and safe loan, designed so that you pay back all that you owe by the end of the mortgage term. Each monthly payment consists of a percentage of both the interest and the capital. In the early years, the majority of your payment will go to repaying the interest; over time, however, the amount going to repay the capital gradually increases. By the end, virtually all of your payments go towards the repayment of capital. The advantages are that it is extremely simple and safe, and you know exactly what you need to pay, where, and when. The disadvantage is that there is no chance for you to make a profit with such a mortgage. If you do run into trouble, then it is easier to negotiate a reasonable solution – such as just to pay the interest and not the capital during the mortgage's term – than with other mortgages.

An Interest-only (Endowment) mortgage

As its name suggests, over the course of the loan you pay interest to your lender, while at the same time you make another payment into an investment which should be worth enough to pay off your mortgage in one lump sum at the end of its term (the standard term is twenty-five years).

How, then, do you amass the money for your lump-sum payment? Traditionally in the UK, people have bought an *endowment*. This is money invested in the stock market – which means it is at risk. But these days there are a whole host of options available, including ISAs, pensions, unit trusts, life assurance schemes and tracker funds. At the end of the day, this all boils down to the same thing, which is that you are investing in the stock market in the hope that by the time you have to repay the building society your investment will be worth as much, or possibly more, than what you owe them. In a worst-case scenario, when the securities are under-performing, you may not have enough money to cover the endowment principal at the end of the mortgage. In this case, you will need to find the money elsewhere – perhaps by selling your house.

In the case of either of these types of mortgages, you should look out for penalties for early or late payment. Ask whether penalties exist. If so, ask your lender to show you exactly where on the contract penalties are explained. Then make sure you have a clear understanding of the amount of the penalties, and how they are triggered. Do not sign the contract until you understand what the terms are.

The UK has one of the most competitive mortgage markets in the world. That gives you a huge advantage. Most lenders are desperate for your business, and if you don't find what you want, don't be afraid to shop around and negotiate. You have the power now, and as Obe Wan-Kenobe might say, 'Let the force be with you.'

How Much Mortgage Do You *Really* Pay?

Example 1: a £60,000 repayment loan, at 6.99 per cent for a ten-year-term loan:

Monthly payment	£694.08
Total amount payable:	£83,289.60

Example 2: a £100,000 repayment loan, at 6.99 per cent over a twenty-five-year-term loan:

Monthly payment:	£696.97
Total amount payable:	£209,091.00

Example 3: a £80,000 repayment loan, at a low start of 6.29 per cent for the first five years and then at 6.99 per cent for the remaining twenty years:

Monthly payment at 6.29 per cent	£520.25
Monthly payment at 6.99 per cent	£548.95
Total amount payable:	£162,962.40

(*Source*: Halifax)

The most important thing you need to concentrate on is the interest rate and penalties associated with a mortgage. The interest rate is *the* key figure: over the life of a twenty-five year mortgage, with an interest rate of about 9 per cent, you will pay some £120,000 of interest for a mere £40,000 loan.

The other big question is whether you would prefer an interest-only or repayment mortgage. Once you've decided, you'll be offered a sometimes bewildering number of variations on these two themes, which I've explained in simple terms below.

Common types of mortgages

1) *Variable Rate mortgage*: the interest rate on your mortgage goes up and down with other interest rates set by the mortgage lender: as a result, your payments vary. If interest rates rise, your mortgage payments increase; if they decline, your payments decrease. For variable rate mortgages, banks and building societies are often quick to add higher interest rates to payments, but are slow to incorporate lowered interest rates.

2) *Fixed Rate mortgage*: the interest rate, and your monthly payments, remain constant for a fixed amount of time. By shopping around you can find everything from a six-month fix to the whole life of the mortgage, and everything in between. This is the ideal option if you need certainty about what your monthly payments are going to be. But bear in mind that you're gambling that interest rates will remain at the level you have fixed, or higher.

In 1992, one friend took a gamble with a five-year fixed rate of 10.5 per cent. This was lower than mortgage rates had been in the last twelve years and he anticipated that they wouldn't sink any further. Since then, in fact, mortgage rates have never risen *above* 10.5 per cent. My friend lost his bet – but has no real regrets, because he was on a tight budget when he bought the house and needed to know *exactly* what his monthly outgoings were going to be.

3) *Capped mortgage*: this is a half-way house between a variable-rate and a fixed rate mortgage. A capped mortgage means your interest rate is 'capped', or guaranteed, not to go above a certain figure.

4) *Discount mortgage*: gives you a discount on the variable rate set by your bank; so whatever that rate is, you get a discount on it. The percentage of discount and the variable rate differs from bank to bank, so be sure to shop around for this type of mortgage.

5) *Low Start mortgage*: as its name suggests, this mortgage starts off with a low interest rate which then increases substantially over three to five years. The idea is that by the time interest rates have risen, so will your take-home pay. A few years ago, low start mortgages were sold heavily, on the notion that you could put future earnings to work for you today – in other words, buy your dream now and pay for it later. The problem with low start mortgages is that if the salary increase you hoped for never materialises – or you lose your job – then you will find yourself in a tight spot. Not surprisingly, the bloom is off this type of mortgage.

Other types of mortgages

The kinds of mortgages listed above determine the interest rate you will pay in differing ways. In addition, you may have two other mortgage options to consider.

1) *Cash-back mortgage*: gives you a loan that covers the property, and also puts cash in your hands. While such a mortgage can give you the impression that you've been handed free cash, in reality you will be carrying more debt. Many people use this 'cash back' to furnish their home. But ask yourself if the added debt burden is really worth it. Could you bear to eat off cardboard boxes draped in muslin sheets for a year? It might be worth the sacrifice.

2) *Flexible mortgage*: allows you to make additional payments on the principal or capital of your mortgage, and thereby shorten the term of the loan. In effect, you are using your extra mortgage payments to save money. Some of these mortgages allow you to build up a reserve, which you can draw down from or even withdraw at a later date. Also, flexible mortgages allow you to temporarily suspend your mortgage payments if you need to.

A Reduced Mortgage Term Equals Big Savings

By reducing the repayment period of your mortgage loan, you can reduce the amount you will pay over time. With an interest rate of 6.5 per cent, for example, and an average loan of £60,000, this is how the sums work out:

Term	Monthly payment	Total payable	Interest	Saving
25 years	£393.65	£118,095.00	£58,095.00	nil
20 years	£437.53	£105,007.20	£45,007.20	£13,087.80
15 years	£515.51	£92,791.80	£32,791.80	£25,303.20
10 years	£679.27	£81,512.40	£21,512.40	£36,582.60
5 years	£1,186.93	£71,215.80	£11,215.80	£46,879.20

Hidden costs of home ownership

Don't lose sight of the fact that the purchase price is only part of the cost of a new home. Aside from the deposit, you'll also need to pay for such things as a solicitor, valuation, surveys, conveyancing, stamp duty, arrangement fees and insurance, the cost of buying appliances from existing tenants and moving costs. Indeed, you can be sure that for as long as you own a home you will be paying for *something* – new furniture, old boiler, leaky pipes – at all times.

BEWARE THE 'PERFECT WALLPAPER' TRAP

The temptation of most first-time home buyers is to put their personal aesthetic stamp on a home, and to make it 'perfect' as quickly as possible. Often this results in design decisions that are only meaningful, and logical, to themselves.

Common Costs of Buying and Selling a Home

House cost:	£50,000	£100,000
Stamp duty	nil	£1,000
Solicitor's fees	£600	£900
Searches	£25–£150	£25–£150
Land registery	£80	£80
Lender's valuation	£110	£160
Survey fee (basic)	£300	£300
Buildings insurance	£100	£200
Removal firm	£300	£300

Most UK houses are sold empty. If you want to buy curtains, carpets or electrical appliances you usually have to negotiate at the point of making an offer on the property. There may also be small charges to change the subscriber's name on telephone lines and cable TV but these are changing all the time and vary enormously from one company to another. Some sellers even try and take away substantial plants and garden ornaments, sheds, greenhouses and so on – or will sell to the buyer in a separate deal.

Of course, if you are selling, there is likely to be the charge made by the estate agent; as of this writing it stands at around 1.5 or 2 per cent, a fee that includes regular advertising in newspapers and on the web. However, if you are selling a substantial house and you want fancy brochures with colour pictures, you're likely to be charged a further £600–£800 in printing costs.

There are ways to avoid these sale charges – for example, one friend recently sold her house by advertising in a national newspaper, at a cost of just £300. Some people even put up their own sales board and wait for buyers to knock on the door.

Finally, don't forget to budget for the many little extra costs incurred in a move – for example reprinting your stationery and changing the addresses on documents such as your passports and drivers' licences.

A friend who is a fan of the Austin Powers movies chose to wallpaper his hallway in a hue and pattern that can only be described as 'Shagadelic, baby!' While it suits him, he is going to have trouble recouping his costs: only someone who shares his psychedelic sensibility will find such groovy ornamentation an attractive feature in a new home. *Oh, behave!*

An even more extreme example of this is a young couple I know who started their married life in a brand-new, fully-equipped home by completely redecorating it. They bought matching 'perfect' furniture for every room in the house at great expense. The husband tried to call a halt to the redecorating Blitzkreig once they had finished the ground floor, but the wife – only half-jokingly – said she 'couldn't *bear* to go upstairs' until that, too, had been paved-over in paisley. The result of this decorating delirium was that two debt-free singles became a married couple with over £20,000 of high-interest debt. This focus on instant gratification is sad and senseless. Indeed, so intent were they on creating their 'perfect' fairy-tale environment overnight, that it never occurred to them that there might be even greater, and far deeper, benefits in building a home together over time. Remember: Rome wasn't built in a day.

Decorating is a lot of fun, but it's expensive and should be undertaken with an eye to the future. Bear in mind that the average first-time homeowner moves after only five to seven years, so chances are you won't be in your first home for long. Whoever buys your place will probably want to re-do it to their own taste.

Make practical alterations to your home, rather than idiosyncratic design statements – especially if it's your first property. This will save you money for the day when you can afford your true dream palace, and will make your property easier to sell.

The Black Hole of Home Improvements

Every year, Britons spend approximately £30 billion on home improvements – although it doesn't always make sense. Over-improving property is rampant here: people routinely spend £50,000 doing up a house worth £100,000 when they know the most expensive similar houses in the area will only fetch £125,000. Indeed, it's estimated that Britons will waste upwards of £10 billion per year on home improvements that fail to increase the value of their homes.

It's easy to get carried away by the desire to make your new home into the palace of your dreams. But if there is any chance that you will resell your place, remember that most people seem to want to move into a nice, boring, bland, safe house with low maintenance and low bills. So, before you order a fancy new kitchen and a marble, heart-shaped bathtub worthy of Zsa Zsa Gabor, take a hard look at your budget – and heed the following words of common sense:

- The additions and extensions that best hold their value are those made in high quality materials to simple designs. A plain, average size kitchen fitted with medium range units will cost £6–8,000. It will probably put that much value on the house in terms of making it presentable for sale. However, the same house with a £40,000 kitchen will not recoup the investment.

  People who are prepared to spend a lot on a kitchen will go into a new house and rip out everything that's there anyway. So if you plan to sell your house, the best solution is to spend a small sum on good-quality units – wood, if possible. Best of all, get the units made by a good carpenter – they'll be better quality than factory made and they'll hold their value.

  Or, choose an unfitted kitchen – that's even more portable.

- The same rules apply to the bathroom. The best investment here is in a simple, good-quality, white suite.
Anything fancy or unusual might be good to live with,
but it won't add to the house value.

- For improving the value of a house retain original design
features, good-quality decoration in plain and neutral
colours, unpatterned carpets or varnished floorboards,
good quality and regularly maintained plumbing and
electrical wiring (with certificates if possible), efficient,
low-energy heating – cleanliness, damp proofing and
wood protection treatments (with certificates).

  A new innovation is the *house log book* – it works just
like a car log book and is a record of all works and
maintenance – it can be sold with the house and is
popular with buyers.

- For reducing the value of a house the worst crimes are
stone cladding to the exterior, plastic UPVC windows,
removing original design features, loud pattern carpet,
bright colours, tacky wallpaper and poor maintenance.

Most Popular Improvements

(Figures based on work done by those carrying out improvements in the year ending summer 1998)

Double glazing	33 per cent
Garden improvements	29 per cent
Fitted kitchen	26 per cent
New bathroom	22 per cent
Central heating	16 per cent

(*Source*: Halifax)

Which Home Improvements Add Value?

Improvement	Cost	Maximum per cent of cost back
(N.B.: These are maximums and depend on your existing house price)		
Off-street parking	£500	200 per cent
Power shower	£400	100 per cent
Central heating	£2,500	80 per cent
Double glazing	£2,500–5,000	50–75 per cent
Conservatory	£6000	70 per cent
Garage	£7000	70 per cent
New fitted kitchen	£5000–10,000	60 per cent
New bathroom	£2,500	55 per cent
Loft conversion	£15,000	50 per cent

(*Source*: BBC *Good Homes Magazine*)

Buy to Let

The popularity of investing in a property specifically to let varies with the economy: during periods when prices are escalating, many people try to tap that vast pool of those who can't, or choose not to, buy themselves. In Britain, such properties are a major source of income for older people who have accumulated a portfolio of such properties over the years. The downside is that such investments often require a lot more maintenance than people are aware of, or want to perform.

High tenant turnover is seldom a good thing. It increases wear and tear and necessitates the replacement of items, or repainting, to keep the place up to standard. This eats into your time and wallet. Turnover also increases the chance that your property will be vacant, in which case you will have to continue to pay the bills without any rental income.

To be prepared, you need to accumulate sufficient reserves to cover replacement costs for everything from basins to boilers, so that the building can continue to generate an acceptable level of income. And reserves must take into account those periods when the property is unoccupied – either due to lack of renters or for necessary repairs.

Before buying a property to let, then, you need to draw up a hard, fast and conservative budget for your income and expenses. Estimate rental income low and maintenance costs high, and always expect periods of losses.

BUILDING AND CONTENTS INSURANCE

After you spend a lot of energy and money on a new home, be sure to protect your investment with building and contents insurance. Building insurance will cover you for the cost of rebuilding your home if it is damaged or destroyed. Contents insurance covers damage or loss of your valuables, clothes, furniture, etc. After all, floods, fires and high winds *do* happen, and burglars or incompetent 'cowboy' workmen are still an annoying fact of life.

REMORTGAGING

Remortgaging describes getting a new mortgage on your property – either by changing from one type of mortgage to another, or switching from one lender to another, both of which you must pay a fee for. You will probably have to pay a penalty for withdrawing from your previous mortgage, but see if you can get your new lender to pick up some or all of the costs associated with your new mortgage – such as solicitor's and surveyor's fees.

If you have a fixed-rate mortgage, for example, and interest rates drop, then you might want to remortgage at a lower rate. (The amount that rates must drop depends on your existing interest rate, the remaining term of your mortgage and your willingness to accept the headache of filing the necessary papers.)

If the value of your property has risen substantially, you can choose to remortgage and pull some of the equity out of your property to pay for other things. Most people use this money to make improvements on their homes, although some use it to pay off other loans, such as high-interest credit card debt.

In the past, home ownership was a form of forced savings – by making your mortgage payments every month, you benefited as the value of your property grew beyond the value of the mortgage. Lately, however, that vision has shifted.

Now we like to think of our home as an investment. People always say, 'I'm *investing* in property,' and they monitor the sale prices of comparable houses and flats more closely than they monitor stock prices. Built into that monitoring, however, is the false assumption that property is as easy to sell and turn into cash as stocks. It is not.

While many people have made money on property, most have done so over the long term, and there are no guarantees. If you are lucky enough to make a profit, consider it the icing on your cake. But remember, what you're really buying is a place you'll enjoy living in for at least the next five years – and often a good deal more.

CHAPTER 6

THE COST OF COMMITMENT: YOUR MONEY AND YOUR LOVE

The Alvin Hall Quick Quiz on Money and Relationships

- Do you think love will solve your money problems?
- Do you avoid talking to your partner about money because 'it's too stressful'?
- Do you believe you can solve your partner's financial problems?
- Do you hide credit card statements from your partner?
- Do you use money from a joint account to buy yourself treats?
- Do you have a child, but no life assurance or a will?

If you answer Yes to three or more of these questions, you may be heading towards a case of the Love and Money Blues. For practical advice on how to avoid this fate, read on.

In a survey of couples by Relate, the marriage guidance counsellor, some 70 per cent of the respondents said that money was the number one cause of arguments in their relationship – even more than sex.

Money is a metaphor for many things, and different people interpret its meaning in different ways: money can provide wings of freedom, but a lack of money can be like a heavy anchor or a chain; money can shield you from life's vicissitudes, but too much money can, ironically, act like a poison. One thing that remains constant, however, is that money is inextricably linked to our self-image and is hard-wired to some of our deepest emotions. Indeed, there are times when the intensity of the feelings that money stirs up is second only to love itself, or lust.

It is not unheard of for a discussion about, say, a credit card bill to veer sharply into an argument about a couple's joint finances, escalate into a shouting match about responsibility and end with a sulking tirade about the mixed joys and doubts of commitment. Such tiffs can be a flashpoint for other hidden tensions in a relationship, and can quickly grow nasty, leading to a further spiral of conflict.

Talk about money, it seems, is the last taboo. Many couples – even those who rarely fight – shy away from openly discussing the details of their finances. But this is a mistake. Learning to talk about money, especially about joint finances, is one of the most difficult but important challenges in sustaining a relationship.

Frank financial conversation allows you to get to know your partner intimately, warts and all, and forces you to consider your own strengths and weaknesses.

In the best case, money can lead to a deeper intimacy and empathy with your mate. There are times, after all, when we all need a shoulder to lean on.

Talking about money – how you get it, save it and spend it – with your partner is essential for a healthy relationship, even in the worst of times. Conversely, a lack of money talk can lead to resentment, suspicion and even skulduggery.

I know a young married couple where the husband is eager to talk about money but the wife has always been reticent. Frustrated over the fact that he didn't know what his wife was worth, the husband tried some amateur sleuthing. Unearthing her bank statements and pay stubs, he pieced together a financial picture of his wife. What he discovered was that she is a hoarder, and is, in fact, worth quite a lot. With a certain amount of hurt, he realised that she had shielded the truth about her finances from him, at least in part, because she was worried that he might use her for her money. When I questioned the wisdom of his snooping, he said that for the sake of harmony in their marriage he had decided not to mention it. After all, he admitted, his wife is not really hurting anyone with her secretive saving. But I know that he still resents her secrecy, and I wouldn't be surprised if they had further arguments over family finances.

Another big danger is what I think of as the 'Broken Wing Syndrome', in which one partner *knows* the other has unhealthy spending habits (the bird with the broken wing), but thinks that he or she can fix those problems (mend the wing) and allow their partner to fly free.

Take, for example, the case of a couple I know for whom this has become a problem worsening over time. When Tracie first visited John's home, she noticed that the electricity was out, the phone didn't work and the gas had been cut off. When she asked about the dark house, John just laughed, and said, 'Oh, it's not a problem. I've been travelling lately and didn't pay my bills – it'll be sorted soon.' Tracie, who is scrupulous about her own accounts, thought this was amusing and paid it no attention. But three weeks later, when John's house was still dark, and Tracie discovered several rubbish bags filled with months-old, unopened utility bills, she began to worry. John blithely admitted that he only paid the bills if his creditors called and he happened to pick up the phone. Then it got worse: John had been using his corporate credit card to pay his bills, but had not reimbursed his employer, and his card was suspended. No longer amused, Tracie patiently explained to John why his money habits were unhealthy.

Later, when they moved in together, Tracie believed that she could change John's money personality, and was determined to do so. She put him on a strict, cash-only budget (when we are children, we call this pocket money) which John promptly ignored. He continued to spend like crazy, and even used their joint account to pay for £5,000 worth of gifts for friends. Tracie grew distraught. When I suggested that she simply cut off all funds to John, Tracie said she couldn't – that she cared too much for John and didn't want him to suffer. Tracie had become John's enabler, as they say in the substance-abuse profession, and now, thirteen years into their relationship, John's spending habits are more irresponsible than ever. Clearly, this is not a healthy state of affairs for either spouse. But the pattern has been set and reinforced countless times, and I wonder if it will ever really change.

What are the lessons of this story? First, don't enter a relationship with the assumption that you can change someone's fundamental money personality – chances are you cannot, or that it will take a vast effort to do so, which may, in itself, disrupt the relationship. Second, don't ever allow yourself to become the enabler – the longer you let such a situation go on, the harder it will be to change its patterns. If you are in love with someone who has bad financial habits, and are still prepared to commit yourself, then you need to establish an iron-clad wall between your accounts, and perhaps form an agreement about exactly how your joint monies will be used. Each couple has to work out their own way of communicating. As far as your romantic life goes, it's up to you. But when it comes to talking about your joint financial fortune – whether good, bad or indifferent – it's best to communicate early, honestly and often. Talking about money is never easy; but it is important. Here are a few general recommendations for how to deal with love and lucre:

1) It is important to sit down and talk about your money – ideally before marriage, but also once you are married. Always talk about the facts. Don't assume anything about the attitudes of your beloved. People change, and couples are amazingly secretive about their personal hopes and dreams, even with each other.

   A friend took a job at a huge Wall Street firm hoping to make a lot of money and retire after seven years to teach. His wife, meanwhile, had grown accustomed to their income and was spending like mad. Seven years later, when he realised that her spending would eclipse his plans for early retirement, this couple went through a very acrimonious divorce. When he vented his fury at how she had derailed his plans, she replied: 'You never told me. I didn't know. You don't deserve it [the money].' That's a harsh sentiment, and this is an extreme case, of course, but the lesson is there for all of us to learn from.

2) Be prepared to negotiate: if the husband wants to retire in five years' time, and the wife wants to decorate the house, then they should try to work out an arrangement: perhaps he works for eight years and she decorates only part of their castle.

3) Share your worries and hopes. If money is worrying you, then you should be openly sharing your concerns with your spouse. It shouldn't be the job of one person to shoulder all the responsibility and anxiety.

4) Share the responsibility for managing the family finances. A man I knew had to learn how to balance a chequebook and use a credit card for the first time at the age of seventy, when his wife – who had taken care of all their finances – suddenly died. Another couple I knew split up and the wife was left feeling 'naked' because she didn't even have her own bank account. The lesson is: while one person may do the bookkeeping, you both need to understand how money works.

FOR RICHER OR POORER: GOOD HABITS OF SUCCESSFUL COHABITORS

Here are a few more specific guidelines on money and love:

Full disclosure is the best policy

How should you talk about money? In a word: honestly. You could do worse than setting aside an evening, opening a bottle of wine or brewing a pot of tea, and getting down to the nitty-gritty of talking about money. Pens and paper are helpful, too. Full disclosure is essential.

Among the questions you should ask each other are:

- What is each of you worth?
- How much do you earn?
- What property do you own?
- Do you save? If so, is it regularly or haphazardly?
- Have you ever been in deep financial trouble?
- How much debt are you carrying now?
- What are your biggest financial fears?
- What are your professional and/or financial goals?

You should also talk about your long-term dreams. If you've always thought of opening a florist's shop, taking a year off to caravan around Australia, or learning how to play the flamenco guitar, the sooner you talk about the financial implications of your dream, the sooner you can begin to plan for it. Or, if you have completely different visions – like the husband who wants to buy a sea-kayak and the wife who wants liposuction – the more time you'll have to work through a series of compromises.

The secret about keeping secrets: don't
If you spy on your partner's spending habits, it reveals an underlying lack of trust. And if you don't trust them with money, you'll probably feel the same way about other aspects of the relationship. Similarly, if you hide your bills and receipts, that means you feel guilty about your own spending routines. Neither habit is healthy. The truth will come out eventually (as soon as your partner sees your credit card statement – or, worse, when the bailiff comes to call), and the longer you wait to talk about money the harder it will be to get through it without a row.

All for one, one for all
Once you've started talking openly about your joint finances, make sure you plan ahead *together*. You are in a partnership, after all, and there's no point in one of you saving for the big holiday in Greece if the other is spending the joint savings on nightly take-away binges.

Also, don't fall into the trap of having only one of you work on financial planning. Even if your partner is a financial whiz, you still need to participate in the process. If you were ever to split up – or if one of you dies or is incapacitated – then you should both be equally informed about the financial implications, and your rights.

Joint accounts require rules

A joint bank account is convenient for paying everyday bills and offers other advantages – for example, the fact that funds in the account are not frozen on the death of a partner. However, a joint account sometimes leads to terrible fights between couples, especially if you have different spending habits. Don't assume that your other half knows exactly how you think about money. Sit down and decide which expenditures are to come out of the joint account. Use this account to pay for the shared essentials – mortgage or rent payments, food and utility bills. In the meantime, keep your own account and use it for those other little (or big) extras.

While a joint account may seem like a logical extension of your affection for each other, there are pitfalls: if you split up, dividing the money in the account can be sticky. Who contributed what percentage of the money? After the fact, it's almost impossible to tell. Furthermore, either person has access to *all* of the money in a joint account, and can therefore withdraw it *all* whenever they like – as the following true story demonstrates.

Feeling the entrepreneurial urge, my friend Phil left his important Wall Street job and started his own firm; as a result, he had to cut back on his spending. His wife Lila missed the perks of their former life, and was unhappy with the direction he was taking his career. Claiming an incredible series of headaches, backaches and other unlikely maladies, Lila punished Phil by withholding her considerable charms from him . . . for six months. Phil is a man of great energy and pride, and after a while he grew incurably frustrated; so he began an affair with a strict, kinky woman. Lila began to suspect.

One afternoon, Phil snuck his mistress into a room in his private men's club (where women are strictly forbidden). Lila appeared in the lobby of the club in a state: she was 'worried' about her husband, she told the concierge, he had recently 'lost' his job and had been 'acting strangely'; she thought he might be despondent and attempt suicide! Alarmed, a guard rushed upstairs with her. Bursting in on Phil and his lover, adrift in a post-coital stupor, Lila shrieked 'Betrayal!' Then she went directly to the bank and emptied their joint account – which was his only savings. Phil – broke, divorced and *persona non grata* at his favourite club – had hit the comeuppance trifecta. (If he'd had his own bank account, of course, he would have only had to worry about two out of three strikes against him.)

Not only is it financially wise to maintain separate accounts, it's also better *emotionally*, to allow each partner a certain amount of latitude. Money can be used as a means of control. Think about some of the traditional, unequal relationships our parents and grandparents endured: men tended to dominate financially and, as a result, even when the husband was thoughtful, generous and kind to his wife, many women felt dependent, insecure and afraid to air their feelings openly. Joint control of money leads to an open, healthier relationship in general.

As a way to compromise, consider putting only a percentage (that you both agree on) of your savings and earnings into the joint account, and the rest into your individual accounts. In this scenario, you have the freedom to save or spend your money as you like to. After all, most people feel comfortable having a certain amount of their own spending money – 'mad money', some call it – even if they have a joint account with a partner.

If you do decide to share an account, you will need to develop a system to keep track of your spending, so that you won't unexpectedly run dry. A good way to do this is to appoint one person the household banker. My friends Nick and Sara, for example, put all of their household bills, receipts, ATM bank withdrawal slips and cancelled cheques into a file. Once a month, Sara goes through the file, pays the bills and balances their joint account.

Separate but equal

Don't allow yourself to be pressurised into guaranteeing your partner's loans or paying off their debts – at least not on any kind of regular or repetitive basis. There's no point in both of you losing everything if it all goes awry.

Sadly, these kinds of stories are as old as dirt. I know a couple, for instance, who got married and set up house: six months into the marriage, his car broke and she guaranteed the purchase of a new car. Six months after that, the relationship had soured and he simply drove away in the new car. She was left with a broken heart, his broken old car and in debt. People like to think this kind of story is reserved for soap operas and Country and Western songs, when in fact it happens all the time – particularly in the early stages of a relationship, when love and trust are new.

In a second marriage, those who have been through a divorce may choose to keep their assets totally separate, in order to protect themselves should they ever have to divorce again. This is a personal choice. But for the sake of your marriage, don't hide money from one another, and don't use money to control your partner.

Co-ordinate your employer benefits and insurance needs

Educate yourself on what kind of benefits your and your partner's job gives each of you, and how to make best use of them. Using the best that each package has to offer can increase your combined savings – significantly – in the long run. One of you may have an excellent pension scheme, for example, while the other may have a superior health-benefits plan. Increasingly, large companies often offer their employees a 'menu' of benefits, from which employees can pick and choose; this cuts down on needlessly duplicating benefits. It may seem boring, but it is worth your while to understand how to make your employer-sponsored schemes work best for both of you.

Informal living relationships shouldn't lead to informal financial relationships

Millions of lovers and flatmates are now sharing homes without the benefit of any legal bond. But this is no excuse for ignoring the fiscal realities. Here are a few common-sense suggestions for uncommitted cohabitors:

- Each of you should be responsible for personal expenses, and work out a joint system for paying household bills.
- If you buy a property together, you should sign a *Cohabitation Agreement*. This will lay out legally, on paper, how expenses such as mortgage payments, taxes and insurance are paid – and what happens if the property needs major work, or you split up. Have a lawyer draw up the agreement for you.
- Each of you should have a will drawn up, to ensure that your property goes where you want it to go in the event of your death. (This is particularly important if your family disapproves of the relationship. Nothing can be more heartbreaking than for the shock of an unexpected death to be worsened by fights over inheritance and the financial hardships that may result.) Again, this is a matter for a lawyer.

Love is about give and take

Money is only part of the whole equation of your life together, and each of you should contribute however you can. Your contributions should be fair to each of you, depending on circumstances.

Bill payments, for example, don't need to be split strictly down the middle: a fifty-fifty split may work only if you are both earning about the same amount of money. If you earn 60 per cent of the joint income, then maybe you should pay 60 per cent of the joint expenses. If you carry most of the weight of the joint finances – either by putting more away in savings or paying more of the bills – then perhaps your partner should contribute in another way, such as doing more of the shopping, cleaning or child care. After all, an important aspect of the traditional marriage vow is to stand by your other half, 'for richer, for poorer'.

Although there are no hard and fast rules about how to divide your responsibilities, flexibility is important. If an exotic holiday is deeply important to you, then maybe you should pay for a higher percentage of the trip; if the car is a high priority for your spouse, however, then maybe he or she should pay more for it. The question you need to ask each other is: do you both feel, deep inside, that the financial arrangements you've made are fair? Cohabitation is always a series of compromises; if one of you is harbouring an unspoken resentment, it will only grow worse over time.

BUDGETING FOR BABY

Having children is one of the high points of life, but it is also one of the biggest financial commitments you will ever make.

With children in the picture your already precious time, money and sleep will become even more valuable. The cost of things such as baby food, nappies, pram, child care, clothing, toys, car seats, education, insurance, a larger house and a larger car with more insurance add up quickly. And, it's never too soon to start saving for university!

How do you estimate the cost of kids? Alas, there is no simple formula. It's safe (and somewhat obvious) to say that the better you manage your finances, the less tension over your family life there will be.

With that in mind, here are a few tips on preparing for the cost of kids.

The price of parenthood

If you are someone who has had difficulty living within your means before having a child, then be forewarned: food and clothing expenses will increase at least 10 to 20 per cent, and you're likely to spend more on everything else, too. Indeed, it's been estimated that the first sixteen years of a child's life will cost you a minimum of £68,000

If you want to be an involved parent, you will have less time to earn money. For some people, especially mothers, working at a full-time job will not be possible, or desirable, which will further decrease income.

Even those women who want – or have – to go back to work will find that having kids has cut into their earning power and ability to move up the career ladder. And although it's physically easier to have kids in your early twenties, the younger (and less-educated) a working mother is, the harder parenthood will impact her career. If you give up work in your early twenties to look after your baby, researchers estimate you could lose over *half* your lifetime earnings. If you wait until your late twenties or early thirties, and take the minimum statutory time off (six weeks), you can reduce that loss to about 5 per cent of your lifetime earnings – but even so, it could take another ten years to catch up with your peers.

Furthermore, if you stop work to look after your children, you lose your ability to invest in your pension. If a twenty-six-year-old stops work for six years, it is estimated that she could reduce the ultimate value of her personal pension by a full quarter. Her only recourse is to invest in stocks and bonds for retirement, put money away into an ISA, or have her spouse put more into his pension for both of them.

You can't have it all

As with any other major life decision, having a family requires you to plan ahead. In a financial sense, this means you need to prioritise your goals, start saving with a vengeance and rethink many of your routine spending habits.

Your little bundle of love will force you to answer such questions as: would you rather work hard at a high-powered job in order to afford a large or luxurious home, or work less in order to spend more time with your family? Can you reduce your spending on favourite luxuries such as designer clothes, going out and taxi rides in order to save more?

If you are embarking on the adventure of parenthood, try to leave some flexibility in your plans for future work and income. It's impossible to predict how your partner will feel once you have a child or two. Like any major life change, becoming parents has a way of changing us in unexpected ways: many parents find their interest in work and socialising lessens, and the value of spending time at home increases. Your priorities change with parenthood, and thus your decisions about how to spend time change, too. If that happens, being locked into fixed expenses can be unsatisfying. When a family's finances are structured so that the new mother *has* to return to her job three months after giving birth, for example, she may feel frustrated and resentful.

Maternity (and paternity) leave

All working women, even part-time workers, are now entitled to maternity leave. The minimum your employer has to give you is six weeks off at 90 per cent of your average pay. You are then entitled to another twelve weeks off with a £60.20 per week Maternity Allowance provided by the state. If you have worked for the same firm for one year or more, you are entitled to a total of 29 weeks of leave after birth. However, the weeks beyond those covered by your employer (6 weeks) and the state (12 weeks) are unpaid leave. Remember this is the absolute minimum you are entitled to and if you are lucky your company may be more generous than this. Fathers are entitled to thirteen weeks leave in the first five years of a child's life. If you're self-employed, the rules are different.

You should carefully consider your financial status before taking a leave, and preferably before you become pregnant. The Maternity Alliance (020 7588 8582) is a good source of information and advice.

When mothers return to work

The bottom line is that bosses must not discriminate against working mothers by failing to promote them or by picking on them in times of downsizing. Good employers recognise that women returning to work from maternity leave are a valuable asset to the company – and some firms even offer bonuses for going back to work.

Prepare a will

You should have a will regardless of your circumstances, but especially if you have children. If you had a will before having children, you need to rewrite it to include new family members. If you don't have a will, consult a solicitor and have one written up right now. If you and your spouse should die, you need to name a guardian who will raise your children and a clear statement about your wishes for handing on your property.

Resist temptation, feather the nest

Your child may be given gifts of cash or investments by family and friends. You may be tempted to spend it all immediately on champagne, cigars and baby gear – or, as your child grows, on things such as athletic equipment, art classes, and clothing – but beware of overspending.

Naturally, you want to support your child's interests and introduce them to new experiences. But buying them a bewildering array of toys, for example, can have a deleterious effect. Sadly, some parents overindulge their children with material things – such as cars, mobile phones, lavish holidays, sports tutors, giant-screen television sets and expensive clothing that they will quickly outgrow – at the expense of real communication, life-experiences or affection.

Indeed, I have seen parents create great anxiety when they put their children's short-term desires ahead of the entire family's needs. It is important for both parents and children to distinguish between necessities and treats.

As children grow up, you might consider giving them a weekly allowance, and teach them how to save and spend wisely.

If your child is lucky enough to be given a gift of money, you might invest some of it, to build a lump sum for your child's later use. But saving money on a child's behalf can be tricky. Children have their own tax allowances, but the income from investments you've made in a child's name will be taxed on *your* income, at your highest rate. Your child can receive £100 a year in investment income from money given by each parent (£200 in total) before this rule takes effect. Income that a child gets from investments made by friends and relatives other than parents, however, is the child's.

Here are a few suggestions for building your children's capital for the long term:

Bank or building society accounts
A safe harbour for money earmarked for your child. You can open an account in a child's name, or look into a Young Saver's account. Shop around for the best interest rate.

National Savings' Children's Bonus Bonds
Guaranteed by the state, these bonds are tax-free. The minimum investment is £25; the maximum is £1,000. The bonds earn interest for five-year terms, with a bonus paid at the end, and a new interest rate is set for the next five-year period. When a child reaches twenty-one, a bond stops earning interest.

Friendly Society plans
Mutual insurance and savings organisations run friendly society schemes for their members which offer tax-free savings linked to life assurance. Most providers offer plans for children.

Premium Bonds
A chance to gamble without losing your stake. The minimum purchase is £100, and the maximum prize is £1 million. Prizes are based on a return of about 4 per cent. The winnings are tax-free, but of course there is no guarantee that you will win. However, you can cash in your Bonds at any time to the value of your original contribution without interest.

EDUCATIONAL EXPENSES

All parents want the best for their children, and this especially applies to education. Unfortunately, it is now getting more and more expensive to pay for schooling.

Primary and secondary schools are paid for by the State, but a number of parents I know worry that their child won't learn properly at a state school. On the other hand, they are equally concerned about the high tuition costs of private education. Whether to send your child to a private school is a knotty question that you will have to work out for yourself.

A standard day school will cost something like £5,000 a year per child, and a boarding school can add another £10,000 a year to that. Fees rise about 5 per cent a year and they don't generally include the cost of extras such as day trips, or kitting out your child with uniforms.

There are no easy solutions for surmounting this expense, but what I can tell you is that saving for your child's education is no different from saving for yourself. The hard part is getting started, and sticking to it.

With the introduction of student loans and the end of the student grant, a university education is becoming an increasingly precious commodity: for a three-year university course it is now estimated that a student will need something like £20,000 for living expenses alone; and a longer course – for example architecture, which takes seven years – will cost even more.

The primary expenses are tuition and living costs. The State will help you pay for them, but how much each will cost you depends on factors such as your personal circumstances, the course you choose, income, etc.

Help in paying tuition is means tested, and the sooner you apply for financial support the better your chances are of getting it.

Student loans are available to help defray the cost of housing and food, again based on means. A student loan is a low-interest loan (up to 9 per cent of your income over £10,000) that you start repaying the April after you complete your course. Student loan payments are collected by the Inland Revenue. Even if you don't plan to use all of the money, and as long as inflation is lower than interest rates, it is worth taking the maximum loan allowed and putting it into a savings account that pays a reasonable amount of interest.

Some students are entitled to *scholarships* or extra *grants* – if you are disabled, have dependants, or are training to be a teacher or health professional, for example – that never have to be repaid.

Finally, some colleges will extend you a *hardship loan* if you can prove you are in serious financial difficulty. Of course, this is still a loan and will need to be repaid.

THE PRICE OF DIVORCE, THE PERILS OF BEING SINGLE

Over a third of marriages in the UK now end in divorce.

Sometimes the warning signs are clear from early on, while in other cases a spouse will surprise the other with a request to split up. In either case, divorce is never an easy thing to go through – especially if you have children.

To help steer clear of those shoals, or to navigate on your own once a relationship founders, here are a few survival tips:

Talk is cheap, divorce is dear

To guard against family finances becoming a contentious issue, try to talk about how each of you views money, and likes to use it. A few small tiffs are a lot healthier than harbouring grudges that explode into emotional fireballs. If communication about money (among other things) becomes a real problem, a marital counsellor can be of help.

Divorce is a solution of last resort. Lawyers are expensive, and the process is heart-wrenching. If you conclude that you have no choice but to split up, then you may be forced to learn about money very quickly, and under adverse circumstances.

First, make a list of all the assets and liabilities you and your spouse have. Make sure you get all the financial facts right, including your bank records, pay stubs, statements, and mortgage and loan papers. Second, take a hard look at your list and make sure you understand everything you see there. If it isn't clear, ask questions until it is. Third, begin to prioritise the items on the list that you consider important, or not. Fourth, choose carefully the legal and financial advisers you will need.

Assess your spending needs

As a newly single person you will probably have to make do with less income, and the sooner you figure out how much you will need to live on the better. By making a new budget, you will have a better idea of what a fair settlement will be.

In the meantime, start putting your salary, or part of it, into a separate bank account for yourself. If you want to move half of the cash in a joint account into your own account, be candid with your spouse: explain what you are doing and why. If you own investments together, you may want to sell them and divide the proceeds equitably.

Try not to leave a marriage with your ex-spouse owing you money. If it is unavoidable, make sure you have a simple contractual way to collect what you are owed should the repayment never come.

Review your insurance and retirement plans

If you have been insured by your spouse's company insurance scheme, you must be sure to replicate your coverage once you are divorced.

With changes in your current finances and future needs, you will need to overhaul your pension plan and your will. As women have often taken time away from their career to raise a family, and are likely to be lower paid than their spouses, men often have better pension rights upon retirement. In accordance with the 1995 Pension Act, a court can order a husband's pension scheme to pay the wife part of the pension, but not until he retires (although it stops when he dies). The government is reviewing this legislation, which may change to include pension-splitting, where the wife would be entitled to her own share of the husband's pension in her own right.

Don't make major life changes immediately

Divorce is hard enough to adjust to without having to deal with selling your house or getting involved in a new business or investment straight away. If you can, wait until the emotion has subsided and you have got your life in order before making any other big changes. You'll make better decisions with a cool head.

AGEING PARENTS

There will be a time when your role vis-à-vis your parents reverses: suddenly, you will find they need caring for – they become confused, or their bills need paying, or they are increasingly anxious about medical care – and you are thrust into the role of carer. This can be an awkward transition, and if you already have the responsibilities of a job and a family of your own, it can be overwhelming.

In many communities, there are organisations that offer information and counselling on care for the elderly. Try to take the time – even if it is your precious holiday time – to talk with your parents about their income and debts, find out where they keep important documents like wills and pension schemes, and how you can help them. Speak to their doctors about what kind of care they might need, and think about how to react when they become too frail to care for themselves – should they move in with you, should they hire a nurse to assist them, or should they consider a nursing home? All of these are difficult and expensive choices. A nursing home, for instance, can cost £1,500 a month, at least; to afford this care, many people are forced to sell off their homes.

One of the most difficult subjects to discuss with your parents is their estate. No one wants to talk about their own demise, but it is important that your parents' wills and trusts are in order, and that you are clear about what sort of funeral arrangements they would prefer.

Through filming my television show, *Your Money or Your Life*, I've had the luxury of observing people's daily habits up close, and I'm always struck by the anxiety caused when we begin to talk about money. Among the people on our programmes are a few extreme cases – those who view any discussion of money as a personal judgement or threat, or those who literally run away from any hint of financial truth-telling – but the fact is we all recognise parts of ourselves in their stories.

Often, the people on the programme have patterns of spending, or neuroses about money, that were set early in life by their parents. In many cases, these foibles have affected them in some unfortunate way – be it stress in a marriage, bitterness about an inheritance, frustration over a job, excessive worry, or reckless spending habits.

Is there a healthy balance? Well, yes, in this case there is. This is one of those situations where honest conversation can produce practical results. This doesn't mean you should shout out of the window about the details of your credit card debt, of course. But within a family, or a relationship, it is good to make everyone aware of where money comes from, where it goes and what sacrifices are required to attain important goals.

I have friends in New York, for example, who like to send their children to camp during the hot summer months. They are not a wealthy family, but they communicate admirably about money. When the time comes to decide which children will go to which camp, the whole family sits down to discuss what the costs will be for each option: the parents don't use this discussion to make their children feel guilty about spending money; rather, they use it as a teaching tool – the kids understand the costs of camp, help to decide which options make sense, and appreciate their experiences all the more for it.

If only *all* family money discussions could be this harmonious!

In my family, it was my grandmother – who had a very practical view of money – who set the tone. Her attitudes are perhaps best summarised by the way she approached her own funeral. As she neared death, she decided she wanted to put all of her affairs in order *before* she was gone – both so that the job would be done right, and so that she would not burden the family. She set a funeral budget, and invited the rest of us to help her choose her grave-site, coffin, clothes, church, music and choir. (The choice of headstone she left to me.) When everything was organised and paid for, right on budget, she felt a great sense of satisfaction. 'All you have to do now is show up to my funeral,' she said to the family.

Looking back, I see that my grandmother passed on certain values, and an approach to money, that has withstood the test of time. And now it is up to us, the next generation, to pass that knowledge on in our own ways.

CHAPTER 7

EVERYTHING YOU WANT TO KNOW ABOUT INVESTING, BUT ARE AFRAID TO ASK

The Alvin Hall Quick Quiz on Investing

- Do you consider the words 'investing' and 'gambling' to be synonymous?
- Do you like to take risks and invest for the short term on impulse and rumours in the hope that you'll 'strike it rich'?
- Do you invest sums at random, whenever you happen to have a few extra quid on hand?
- Do you have only a vague idea of how you want your money to work for you?
- Do you believe you can consistently outsmart the investment markets?
- Do you tend to dwell on missed investment chances – 'the ones that got away'?
- Does your pride, or delusion, prevent you from selling an investment on which you have lost money?
- Do you spend your dividends as quickly as you earn them?
- Do you try to 'time' the market, to sell as it reaches its peak and buy back when it hits bottom?
- Do you think the price of a stock, after a quick runup, can never go higher?

If you answered 'Yes' to six or more of the above questions, then you need to re-evaluate your investing ideas today.

'**I** work hard to earn my money, and now I want to invest it in the stock market so it will work better for me,' my friend Nigel, a newly-successful computer programmer, said the other day.

When I asked him exactly how he plans to make his money 'work better' using stocks, he answered, with great confidence: 'Always buy low and sell high.'

At first blush, this old chestnut sounds perfectly reasonable. Nigel has saved money above and beyond what's required to cover his basic living expenses, mortgage, insurance, pension and emergency fund; now he wants to use some of this 'extra' money to earn more than it would in a traditional savings account. But, like most neophyte stock investors, Nigel's aspirations are far too general. He has given too little thought to his *investment plan*, which requires him to define specific investment goals, and devise a clear plan to achieve them.

Nigel is not alone. Generally, when people discover they have 'extra' money (often for the first time in their lives), their initial impulse is to run out and spend it as quickly as possible. If they manage to contain that urge, and consider investing instead, their next impulse is to invest in a get-rich-quick scheme. This is an emotional response to good fortune, and it usually results in lost opportunities for real, long-term wealth building.

Before making any kind of significant investment – whether in stocks, bonds, fine art, vintage wine or even ostrich farming –

you must first make a cool-headed evaluation of your current financial status, the reason you are making the investment, what you'd like to achieve with the investment, and the time span for the investment. Then design an appropriate strategy.

The questions listed below are designed to help you think through your plans before you invest a single penny.

IS INVESTING FOR ME?

Despite what many people seem to think, 'saving' and 'investing' are not the same thing. Saving means that you put your money away in a safe, risk-free place. Investing means that you put your money in a business or endeavour in which you could lose your money; in short, investing involves risk. When you invest, not only will the value of your investment fluctuate from day to day, but when you sell the investment you may get back less money than you originally put into it. In a worst-case scenario, you'll get back absolutely nothing.

People interpret the risk of investing in very different ways. At one end of the spectrum there are those for whom even the idea of losing money makes them green around the gills. At the other end, there are those who find the ups and downs of the market as thrilling as a ride on the Big Dipper at Blackpool Pleasure Beach. Most of us are somewhere in between these two extremes, which makes judging risk difficult, especially when the market is moving strongly upward.

Indeed, in America these days, there is such a mania to invest that people feel they are missing the boat if they are not 'playing the stock market'. And I sense this same pressure building in Britain: friends who didn't know – or care – what the stock market was five years ago, now frequently ask me what I think about certain esoteric stocks that they are thinking of risking their money on.

Investing Myths

1) Investing = constantly buying and selling securities
2) Investing = saving
3) The price of a stock can never go higher
4) You must have *lots* of money to invest in shares
5) There is a big secret to investing, and you're not in on it

If the possibility, however remote, of losing a significant portion of your investment makes you tense and queasy, then clearly investing is not for you. However, history has shown that carefully chosen investments, made for the long term, can be a good way to make your money grow faster than it ever would in a conventional bank or building society savings account.

New investors often enter the stock market thinking they will make a killing. Instead, a large percentage get killed and lose most of the money they have invested. Indeed, investing isn't easy for anyone. None of us has a reliable crystal ball, and it's always difficult to read the future. Consider, for example, the recent pace of change in the computer industry.

In the mid-1980s, International Business Machines (IBM) was considered a 'blue-chip' stock – that is, one of the strongest companies in the world (whose total market value was larger than the entire West German stockmarket), and one of the safest investments around. In 1987, its stock was trading as high as $175 7/8 (£106) a share. But as the company failed to adapt to the rapidly changing computer business, its sales and profits stopped growing, and soon IBM's stock plunged. By 1994, it was trading for a mere $40 5/8 (£24) a share, which represented an astounding 77 per cent drop in value in only a few years. (Today, IBM has reinvented itself as a computer-services company and has regained some of its clout.)

Meanwhile, in December 1986, at precisely the moment that

IBM was soaring towards its apparent zenith, the mother of a friend of mine – a woman who liked to invest in stocks for fun – called me and said: 'I've just met the most wonderful young man in Seattle. His name is Bill Gates, and you *must* buy shares in his little company. It's called Microsoft.' Today, of course, Microsoft is the world's most successful software company, and Bill Gates is the richest person in the world, worth a reported $80 billion (£48 billion). But at the time, he and Microsoft were virtually unknown.

If you were me, would you have taken my friend's advice? Remember, it was quite risky at the time. Let's imagine I did.

In December 1986, shares in Microsoft were selling for $48 apiece. If I had bought a hundred shares, and held on to all of that stock until autumn 1999, my $4,800 investment would have increased exponentially: I would have owned some 14,400 shares, worth some $1.224 million (£765,000), close to at their highest price in 1998. That is what investment professionals call a very nice return. So, did I take my friend's advice and buy Microsoft stock in 1986? And did I sell, capturing my million-dollar gain, before all the trouble began (such as the anti-trust lawsuit)? I'm not telling.

Capitalism isn't always fair, but it is the economic system that best accommodates most human impulses – including the willingness to risk losing £10 for the chance of earning £30. Indeed, it is rare in our marketplace for a passive pessimist to triumph. If you are seeking to make a good profit from your money, you must be willing to learn what you are buying, accept the risks inherent in the market and be realistic about the time-frame required to meet your goals.

Ultimately, it's up to you to decide what sort of risk and reward (or anxiety versus profit) balance you are comfortable with. After all, it makes no sense to speculate on any investment – particularly in highly volatile stocks – if you're going to spend all of your gains on anti-ulcer medications and sleeping pills.

HOW MUCH CAN I AFFORD TO INVEST?

The amount of money you'd *like* to invest may not match the amount you actually *can* or *should*, invest. The only money you should consider investing is money you can afford to place at risk: that is, 'extra' funds – money above and beyond your cost of living allowance, emergency reserves, pension and savings you want to keep perfectly safe.

What is the most common mistake people make when trying to determine how much they can afford to invest? They fool themselves. They think that *any* bit of extra money they can lay their hands on – even funds they know deep-down they should be putting into their savings – is fair game. This is a pervasive, and dangerous, delusion. Many people, especially enthusiastic first-timers, often put too much of their money at risk in the stock market – with predictably sad results.

The second most common mistake is that investors let 'experts' help them to fool themselves. Just because a professional suggests you invest a certain amount of money, doesn't mean you have to take his or her advice. Feel free to question the amounts a broker or financial planner suggests; after all, it's not his or her money that's at risk, it's *yours*.

Despite the temptation to try to make a killing in the market, always keep this mantra in mind (you do not have to assume the lotus position while chanting): 'I will invest no more money than I can afford to lose.'

HOW DO I GET STARTED?

If you are to have a reasonable chance of achieving your dreams, you need to state clearly what your investment goals are. This is

How to Determine Your Net Worth

Assets

Cash in current account   £_____
Cash in savings account   _____
Current value of pension scheme   _____
Cash value of life assurance policy   _____
Market value of house or flat   _____
Market value of other property   _____
Market value of Securities:
   Stocks   _____
   Bonds (including Gilts)   _____
   Unit Trusts   _____
   Other   _____
Value of possessions:
   Car   _____
   Household furnishings   _____
   Household appliances and equipment   _____
   Furs and jewellery   _____
   Precious metals   _____
   Collectibles   _____
   Recreation and hobby equipment   _____
Loans receivable   _____
Interest in a business   _____
Other assets   _____
               Total Assets: _____

Liabilities

Unpaid bills   £_____
Credit card balance   _____
Car loan(s)   _____
Taxes due   _____
Balance due on mortgage(s)   _____
Other loans   _____
Other liabilities   _____
          Total Liabilities: _____

Summary:
  Assets:
  Minus liabilities: _____
Your net worth =   _____

important because you will use the statement of your goals both as a guide to the right types of investments for you, and as a benchmark against which to measure the performance of those investments.

Of course, the ways people with similar financial profiles choose to invest their money are as varied as their fingerprints. A person whose goal is to generate income she can use in the near future might want to purchase stocks that pay high dividends. A person whose goal is to build up money for retirement twenty or more years in the future, on the other hand, may invest in stocks with long-term growth potential. A third person may have some extra 'fun' money and decide to speculate on stocks whose prices fluctuate widely in the short term, in the hopes that he will make a few pounds' profit.

To devise an investment plan, follow the steps below and decide what kind of strategy works best for you.

Step One: determine your *net worth* – your financial assets minus your liabilities. To accomplish this, tally up the value of all your assets (for example, your home, possessions, savings and investments) and then subtract your total liabilities (for example, mortgage, car loan, credit card and student loan debts): the result is your net worth. The greater your net worth, the greater your real wealth.

If you are honest in your calculations (please consult the chart opposite), figuring your net worth gives you a direct way of knowing whether you are being realistic about your major financial goals, such as buying a home, riding out unexpected disasters and retiring in comfort. Furthermore, the process of reviewing your accounts will help you to figure out how much 'extra' money you can afford to invest (and lose) in potentially lucrative but risky securities, like stocks, bonds and unit trusts.

Step Two: decide what kind of investment you'd like to make. There are two essential choices: you can become a lender or an owner.

- You are a *lender* when you invest in a *bond*, which is basically an IOU. You lend a sum to a company or the government: the borrower promises to pay you interest on specific dates over the fixed term – say, five, ten or twenty years – and at the end of the term, will repay your original investment, the bond's face value. Bonds are more risky than bank or building society savings accounts (see below), but give you a decent return without the radical ups and downs of the stock market.

- You are an *owner* when you invest your money in an asset, such as shares of a company's *stock*, that allows you to share in the growth and profits of the company. In effect, you become a part-owner of any company in which you own shares – usually a very small part, of course, but a part-owner none the less. And this entitles you to some of the benefits as the company prospers.

  Ownership of a company's shares is referred to as having 'equity' in a company; hence, stocks are called *equity securities* (while bonds, which are loans to a company, are called *debt securities*).

Beneath these two umbrella terms, there are so many different ways of investing your money that the multiplicity of choices can, at times, seem overwhelming. But as I said in the Introduction, there is no reason to be afraid of the market. Things like stocks and bonds are not all that mysterious in the end. If choosing a specific stock or bond is something you're just not interested in, then a good way to get started is to invest in a unit trust – which lessens your risk by pooling the money of many people and investing it in a number of different securities.

Three Common-sense Investing Tips

1) Develop some knowledge of a company before buying its stock.
2) Learn about the company's management – its strengths and weaknesses.
3) Try 'paper investing' – watch the stock's movement over a period of time, learn how the stock responds to news and market conditions, and learn to recognise what types of news affect the stock.

WHAT SORT OF INVESTMENTS SHOULD I CONSIDER?

Once you have built up reserves beyond the money you need for daily and emergency expenses, you will be ready to grow your money in one or more of the investment vehicles described below:

Low-risk investments: bonds

When you invest in a bond issued by a company such as ICI or BT, or a *gilt* (gilt-edged bond) issued by the government, you are lending your money to the bond issuer. In return, you'll be paid a fixed rate of interest (the *coupon*) at regular intervals (i.e. monthly or annually), for a specified period of time (the *term*). At an agreed date, the gilt or bond matures, and the issuer reimburses your original investment (the *principal*).

Bonds are not entirely risk free – companies do go bankrupt, after all, and when they do, they may not pay off their debts. And there have been rare instances of governments defaulting on their loans – as with the Russian government's suspension of debt payments in 1998. Far more often than not, however, you will be paid all of the interest and principal you are due, on time. This makes bonds a relatively safe, or low-risk, investment.

Another risk of investing in bonds is known as *market risk*. This is the risk that the market value of bonds will change as interest rates change. As interest rates rise the market price of any bond will fall because investors can achieve similar returns in less risky savings accounts. Conversely, as interest rates fall, the price of bonds will rise. (These changes of market value will be reflected on your statement.) For most investors day-to-day market risk is of little concern: they hold the bonds to maturity, at which point the issuer will repay the principal in full.

A third risk that affects bonds is called *inflation risk* – the tendency of prices to increase over time, resulting in a reduction in the buying power of your money. For example, let's say you bought a plate of fish and chips on the day you invested in bonds, and the meal cost £2.20. Ten years later, when your bonds mature, and the issuer repays your principal, that same fish and chips might cost you £4.95: this means that, thanks to inflation, your money has lost about half its buying power. Your money is now worth less than when you originally invested it.

Yet, despite these worries, bonds remain one of the most popular investments. People like bonds because they know exactly the interest they will be paid over time, and exactly the amount of principal they will be repaid at maturity.

Gilts (short for gilt-edged securities), also called *Government Bonds*: these are bonds issued by the British government to raise money. As with other bonds, gilts pay a fixed interest rate (the coupon) for a set term, and then return your money on a specified date, known as the redemption date. Gilts are traded on the stock market, and, like bonds, their rates fluctuate according to interest rates: if interest rates drop, gilts rise in value, and vice-versa. Gilts are very safe investments because the government has never defaulted on its payments; their volatility is not a significant issue.

The par value of each gilt stock is £100: this is the sum you will be paid back if you hold the gilt to maturity. Regardless of what price you paid for it, at the maturity date you will only get back par value (£100). The life of such government bonds is usually five, ten or fifteen years, and they are available through a stock-broker or a bank.

Moderate-to-high-risk investments: stocks

When a company 'goes public', or 'has a flotation', it sells its shares of stock – a part ownership of the company – to the public. The shares are traded on a stock exchange. A company issues stock when it wishes to raise capital: this money is earmarked for a specific purpose, such as building new facilities, developing new products, or acquiring other companies.

When you buy shares of stock, there are two ways you can expect to make money: *cash dividends* – a certain amount of a company's after-tax earnings that its board of directors decides to distribute to shareholders and *capital gains* – the profits made when you sell a stock at a higher price than you paid for it. The combination of your dividends and capital gains is called your *total return*. (Stocks do not pay interest, like a bond or a savings account does.)

The amount of money you pay for one share is called the stock's *market price*. A stock's price is dependent upon forces of supply and demand, which are in turn influenced by several factors, each of which has a psychological component:

- The amount of dividend payments: if a company pays higher dividends than the professional analysts expected, then more people buy the stock, and the market price of each share rises. Any cut in a company's dividends, however, is viewed as a sign of weakness; at any hint of such a move, nervous investors will frequently sell their shares, which drives a company's stock price down.

- Expectations of earnings: on a half-yearly basis, analysts predict what they believe a company's earnings will be. For better or worse, these predictions become benchmarks against which a company's performance is measured. If the earnings exceed the analysts' expectations, the company's stock price rises – sometimes strongly. If earnings only match, or fall slightly below, the analysts' predictions, the shares' market price usually declines – as investors sell, hoping to avoid future pitfalls.
- Expectations of increased turnover and/or market share: this is the key measure for many young companies that pay no dividends and have no earnings, such as Internet and biotech stocks. Simply put, investors believe that if such a company's turnover continues to grow, it will eventually show substantial earnings and pay generous dividends. In other words, investors buy an unproven stock today in the hope of benefiting handsomely from its growth tomorrow. However, the stock of these young, unproven companies can be highly volatile. Investors can expect the share price to move wildly up and down, producing a graph that resembles the ECG chart of an impending heart-attack victim – perhaps the investor himself!

Shares *are* risky investments, but they do not all carry the same degree of risk. The kind of shares you can buy ranges from 'blue chip' stock, named after the most valuable poker chip, to 'penny' stock, so-called because they are low-priced.

Investment Wisdom

1) Stick with your basic investment approach; refine it, rather than change it, over time.
2) The market can be cruel to even the most experienced investor. You should be prepared for this, and make it part of your overall investing philosophy.
3) Don't over-invest. By putting too much money on the line, and giving yourself too many choices, you are only going to hamper your ability to make intelligent decisions under pressure.
4) Ignore day-to-day fluctuations in the price of your stocks. Invest for long-term gains.
5) Never 'marry' a stock. Your vow to a stock you are enamoured of should be: 'I promise to stick with you in sickness and in health, for richer or for poorer, for the long term . . . until something better comes along.' In other words, don't develop an emotional attachment to your investment; think about it objectively, and monitor it. After all, good investments can turn bad.

Blue chips are the shares of large, well-established companies – such as ICI or BT – that steadily increase turnover and have consistently paid dividends. The risk of losing your investment in this type of company is relatively low because of its size, product line, diversity and good management. On the other hand, as an owner of ICI stock you won't be able to swagger into a cocktail party and boast of one-day gains worthy of Gordon Gekko.

If swaggering and tremendous gains are part of your investment objective, then more risky stocks are for you. Many people, even conservative investors, are attracted to penny stocks, the shares of small companies with a new idea, or companies that have fallen on hard times. This type of investing can more accurately be described as speculating.

In the investment game, *speculation* is the word for the short-term, high-stakes trading of shares solely to make as much money as possible as quickly as possible. Speculators tend to focus on highly volatile sectors (for example, Internet and emerging technology stock), stock in companies that may become takeover targets, and little-known companies whose prospects are difficult to predict. Unless you are very experienced, wealthy, or simply mad, you should steer clear of speculation.

The groupings of stock are often described in two ways: stocks that reflect the state of a company's growth – such as income stock – and stocks that reflect the company's reaction to the economy – such as cyclical stock (a company whose fortunes directly reflect the ups and downs of the economy). But these categories aren't hard and fast. Companies are always changing and growing. Today's emerging growth stock could be tomorrow's blue chip.

You can invest in stocks directly by purchasing individual shares through a stockbroker, or indirectly by purchasing shares in a unit trust (see below). But don't believe that picking stocks and following them is easy. In fact, it requires significant effort to research and analyse a company's value – its turnover, earnings, dividend yield, and future growth potential – to determine whether it is worthy of your investment.

Here are a few other kinds of investments to bear in mind:

International stocks: if you want to be adventurous, and broaden your portfolio beyond the UK, you could invest in developed economies such as America, Germany and Japan. Or, you might be interested in *emerging markets* – places with fast-changing economies, such as India, Latin America and Eastern Europe. In these investments you will face a unique set of risks, such as unpredictable currency fluctuations, political risk, a lack of accurate information about companies and the potential for insider-trading. On the other hand, the growth of companies in these dynamic economies can sometimes outpace the growth of British companies in a given time period.

Undoubtedly the easiest way for you to invest in international securities is through a unit trust that specialises in these markets (see below). You get the advantage of having a professional manager select the specific securities in which the fund will invest, and your risk is spread over all the securities in the portfolio. If these markets interest you, and you feel you have the experience to understand them, then you may wish to allocate a portion of your investment money – a general rule is no more than 10 to 20 per cent – to international markets.

Socially responsible investments: if you want to combine your investing with your social and environmental awareness, you should consider investing in companies that try to keep the environment clean, that don't purvey alcohol or tobacco products, that don't test products on animals and are not manufacturers of weapons or military hardware.

Many in the City are sceptical of 'social responsibility' as an investing strategy: this is due, in part, to the fact that financiers are often politically conservative and look askance at what they view as crackpot Leftist notions. Statistically, however, many socially responsible funds perform on a par with more conventional funds. In other words, it is possible to make as much money by following your conscience as it is by following the bottom line.

The risk of investing in stocks, of course, is that if a company's business declines, or the economy turns sour, the value of your stock will plummet too. This does happen – we've all heard of companies that go belly-up, and the overall economy suffers periodic downturns or recessions. Nonetheless, for most people at most times, stocks are a sound investment. In fact, averaging in both good and bad times, and successful companies along with deadbeats, the stock market as a whole has enjoyed an average rate of growth of over 10 per cent annually throughout the past twenty or thirty years – which is not a bad return on your investment.

Unit trusts and investment trusts

Unit trust: a portfolio of securities (stocks and/or bonds) managed by an investing professional, the shares – or units – of which are sold to people whose investing objectives are the same as those of the portfolio. In essence, a unit trust is like a giant investing club run by professionals. When buying into a unit trust, therefore, you are buying a piece of the portfolio. For most novice investors, unit trusts make better sense than trying to buy individual securities on their own. A unit trust provides a low-cost way to gain access to the skills of full-time investment managers, and to diversify your portfolio (thereby lowering the risk associated with any one stock).

Depending on the type of trust, and its investment objectives, the managers will invest in stocks, bonds or other securities. The advantage of this scheme is that it allows you to diversify your holdings with one investment. Because unit trusts are typically invested in dozens of different securities, you reduce the risk associated with any one company in the portfolio – and, thus, your risk of losing money.

Like stock, the value of a unit trust can change daily. If more people invest money in the fund, then new units are issued and the fund grows; if people redeem, or sell, their units, the size of the fund shrinks. The price at which you can buy or sell a unit is called its *net asset value*.

A unit trust can be actively managed, or unmanaged. In an *actively managed* unit trust, an investment manager (or team) makes all investment decisions: your fortune, therefore, depends on the manager's skill. This is particularly important, for example, in international markets where investing practices and regulations can be radically different from those in the UK.

Unmanaged unit trusts– sometimes called *tracker funds*– have a fixed portfolio that is set up to mimic a particular index, such as the FT-SE 100 (Financial Times - Stock Exchange 100, which is based on the hundred largest companies whose stock is traded on the London Stock Exchange). The stocks in the fund, therefore, only change when the composition of the index changes.

While access to professional investment management and diversification are attractive features of unit trusts, their main disadvantage is on-going fees. The often high cost can drag down an investor's return. Before investing in any kind of unit trust, therefore, make sure you know who runs the trust, what their investment objectives are and how much you can expect to pay in charges and expenses.

Investment trust: unlike a unit trust, an investment trust is a public limited company which invests in other companies' shares (the shares of the investment trust are quoted on the stock exchange). Like a unit trust, investment trusts are grouped according to their specialty. There are many variations on the theme: some of these trusts offer a variety of shares with different types of returns – say, shares that give you income but not capital growth, or vice-versa.

Investment trusts have a fixed number of shares issued and outstanding; while the value of the investment trust changes daily, the number of shares will not. As a result, the market value of the investment trust's shares can trade at a *premium* or at a *discount* to the value of the securities in the trust's portfolio depending on demand for the investment trust itself.

Open-end Investment Company (OEIC): referred to by its acronym that sounds like 'oik', an Open-end Investment Company is a type of pooled investment that is similar to a unit trust. Individuals, like you and me, invest their money into a portfolio of securities (primarily stocks and/or bonds) which is managed by a professional portfolio manager. The amount of profit you make from an OEIC is directly proportionate to the percentage of the portfolio that you own. If, for example, you own 1 per cent of the total value of the portfolio and the portfolio rises in value by 10 per cent, then the value of your holding also increases by the same percentage.

The OEICs portfolio has a stated investment objective which its manager must adhere to when selecting the securities which will be bought into, and sold out of, the portfolio. Like a unit trust, the primary advantage of an OEIC is diversification. Because the portfolio consists of the shares of many different companies in various business sections, your investment is protected against stock-specific risk – i.e. the risk that a decline in the value of any one company in the portfolio will have a pronounced adverse effect on your OEIC shares.

The primary difference between a unit trust and an OEIC is reflected in the prices at which you can buy and sell them. An OEIC has a more simplified pricing structure. Each OEIC has only one price, called the *net asset value* (NAV). It is computed at the end of each business day and is based on the closing prices of all the shares in the OEICs portfolio, after all of the associated trading and administrative fees have been deducted. When you want to redeem (i.e. sell) your OEIC shares, you do so at the NAV calculated at the end of the day. When you want to buy OEIC shares, you do so at the NAV plus any sales-related charges. Importantly, the percentage and amount of the sales charges are always disclosed to you.

In contrast, each share of a unit trust is priced like an ordinary share. It has a bid price (the price at which you can sell your trust shares) and offer price (the price at which you can purchase shares). The difference between the bid and the offer prices is known as the spread. Unlike an OEICs sales charge which is known to you, the amount or percentage of the spread varies depending on market conditions.

The simplified pricing of OEICs does not mean that you save

money by purchasing them instead of unit trusts. In fact, the overall percentage of the charges on both products is almost the same. The real advantage of the OEIC price structure is for the company that creates them. It can market OEICs more easily in international markets.

OEICs have been available on the continent and in the US for a long time, but have only recently been made available in the UK. In the US, OEICs are known as mutual funds. Americans have more than $4 trillion invested in mutual funds, which makes them the most popular investment vehicle among individual US investors. Indeed many financial institutions are introducing OEICs in the UK, hoping that they will become as popular here as they are in the US.

Individual Savings Account (ISA): the Government has established a number of tax-free schemes to encourage people to save, the latest of which is an 'ISA', or Individual Savings Account. For many people this will be their first method of saving and/or investing. Understanding an ISA is, therefore, important so that you can take maximum advantage of its benefits.

Like its predecessors PEPs (Personal Equity Plans) and TESSAs (Tax-Exempt Special Savings Accounts) which are no longer available to new investors, an ISA is not an investment in itself. Instead, it is an account with a tax benefit. All gains made on the money you place in an ISA are tax-exempt.

An ISA is also user friendly. Once you open an ISA with a manager or administrator (for example a bank, building society, unit trust company, stock broker, or insurance company), you can contribute or withdraw money without penalty at any time you wish. If it suits your lifestyle and money-management habits, you can regularly contribute a small amount to your ISA, for example, each time you get paid. Or if you come into a substantial amount of money unexpectedly, such as an inheritance (my favourite way to receive money), you can contribute a lump sum up to the maximum amount permitted to your ISA all at once. On the other hand, you can also stop making contributions whenever you wish. Having an account in which I can save easily and regularly, as well as pay no taxes on the gains I made would certainly excite me – in more ways than one – to amass as much money as legally permissible in an ISA.

The money you place in an ISA can be either held as cash (a cash ISA), invested in a single security or unit trust (a stock and shares ISA), and/or used to buy specially designed life insurance (a life insurance ISA). [NOTE: I know death is a subject that most people want to avoid; however, be sure to clarify whether your life insurance ISA does or does not pay a death benefit when you 'pass away', leaving your heirs sad, but richer.] The amount you invest in each of these three 'components' (the Government's term) or 'classes of assets' (the City's term) is set in the ISA regulations and is subject to change. To find out the appropriate amounts, please call the Inland Revenue ISA Helpline on 0845 604 1701 or visit its website, *www.inlandrevenue.gov.uk*.

There are two types of ISAs: a maxi ISA and a mini ISA. Understanding the difference between the two is crucial. While it can only have one manager or administrator, a maxi ISA allows you to invest in each of the three asset classes and gives you flexibility in the amount you can invest, in particular the amount invested in the stocks and shares component. If you allocate less than the maximum amounts to cash and life insurance, then the remainder from these two components can be reallocated to the stocks and shares component. Therefore, if you want to invest more money in shares and/or unit trust than the current legislation permits in a mini ISA, then you must open a maxi ISA.

A separate mini ISA can be opened for each of the three components – a mini cash ISA, a mini stocks and shares ISA, and a mini life insurance ISA. This means that you can have a different manager or administrator for each one. In each mini ISA you can contribute up to the maximum amount specified for the asset class. However, no flexibility is possible. You cannot reallocate

money to a different asset class if you do not contribute the
maximum to a specific asset class. In short, the total amount that
can be contributed to the three mini ISAs equals the maximum
contribution to a maxi ISA, without the flexibility.

To most people, an ISA is an ISA is an ISA, to paraphrase
Gertrude Stein, and they don't want to know any other distinc-
tion. But knowing the difference between a maxi and mini ISA
will prevent you from making an all too common mistake:
opening both a mini and a maxi ISA in the same tax year.

Here's a typical scenario. You go to your building society and in
a moment of guilt and concern, combined with the desire to be
pro-active about your finances, open a cash ISA – which unbeknownst to you is actually a cash mini ISA. Later, in the same tax
year, you go to a unit trust company and open a maxi ISA. Now
you have violated a key part of the ISA regulations. Who cares? Well,
the Inland Revenue does and will disallow the second account
you opened. In any given tax year, you can open one maxi ISA or
three mini ISAs, not both. Once you have opened a mini ISA, you
can only open other mini ISAs for the components to which you
have not contributed. In the situation described above, you could
only open a mini stock and shares ISA and a mini-life insurance
ISA – not a maxi ISA – during the same tax year. So make sure that
in your first flush of enthusiasm to open a cash mini ISA with your
building society that you are not limiting your options should
you want to buy stocks and shares in an ISA later in the year.

Regardless of which option you choose, remember the gains
made on the money you put in an ISA are tax free. Here are some
general guidelines you should keep in mind about the money
you save and/or invest through an ISA:

- If you are using an ISA to accumulate money you will need
  in five years or less, then you probably want to keep your
  money in a cash ISA – preferably a high-yielding account.
- If you are using the money to invest in a unit trust or

shares, it is a good idea to keep the time horizon of your investment in mind. A general rule of thumb holds that the longer you can leave the money invested, the greater the risk you can take. Now this does not mean you should go wild and invest in some dodgy penny shares. Be prudent and invest in quality.

- Monitor the performance of your ISA regularly to make sure you are getting a return that is acceptable to you, given the amount of risk you are willing to accept.
- Always look around for the best low-cost deal you can find. Unlike Viv Nicholson who spent, spent, spent, you should use an ISA and save, save, save!

Alternative investments: collectibles

Some people just can't get excited about stocks and bonds. Instead, their hearts pound at the sight of a Christopher Dresser vase, an antique movie poster, or a case of vintage wine. As a category, these non-traditional investments are known as 'collectibles', a vague word that describes everything from Art Nouveau furniture to first-edition books, old dolls, rugs and stamps and even antique zithers.

My own passion is for fine art photography and antiques, and so I completely understand the impulse to 'invest' in collectibles. And while I've made a good profit from the sale of my artwork, I also have a few items I paid good money for in the 1980s . . . and can't give away today. There are those large abstract paintings by once 'hot, emerging' artists who have since faded into computer programming careers, bits of marquee pottery that have proven to be excellent forgeries and an antique chair that I loved for about six months – for its 'eccentric' charm – and now wish I could sell for even one-third of what I paid for it.

You may wonder why I don't just heave this bric-à-brac into the street. Certainly, I don't expect to be buried with these objects, as King Tut was with his sacred totems. No, in truth I keep them as reminders that no one is immune from bad investments – not even me. After all, as the saying goes, 'the sun doesn't shine on every dog every day'.

Here are a few rules to collect by:

- Rule number 1 is that you must truly love what you buy – because these oddities can sometimes prove difficult to sell, especially when you need the money most, and chances are that you will be living with them for a long time.
- Rule number 2: quality, not quantity, is what counts. Some people snap up every piece of Wedgwood 'drab-ware' they can find, often for absurdly high prices. A better investment would be to buy fewer, more distinctive pieces that will retain (or increase) their value over time.
- Rule number 3: don't underestimate the hidden cost of collectibles – the on-going cost of insurance and storage, for example. These costs can quietly chew up your potential profits.

While investing in collectibles can be wonderful, fun and profitable, I wouldn't put any more than 5–10 per cent of my money into them. After all, you can lose your entire investment as quickly as you drop a bottle of wine on the floor – or as unexpectedly as a certain style goes out of vogue.

A case in point was the Dutch Tulip Craze of 1636. This was a classic case of a limited supply of a precious commodity, Dutch tulips, meeting a frenzied demand: everyone in Europe decided they wanted these beautiful flowers at the same time, speculators drove prices sky-high, fortunes were suddenly made on their trade – and then, almost as quickly, lost. Once the fad had blown over, those same beautiful tulips were selling for one-thousandth of what people had paid for them. The tulips had turned into turkeys.

Indeed, when promised returns on an investment – even one you love to look at – sound too good to be true, they generally are.

True, from time to time a revolutionary new business concept proves to be an amazing success, and turns a few lucky investors into millionaires. In recent years, mobile phones, biotechnology and the Internet have spawned such success stories. But for every big winner, there are hundreds, perhaps thousands, of losers.

- *Alternative Farming:* in Britain a few years ago, the Ostrich Farming Corporation promised investors 300 per cent returns over five years. Some four thousand investors poured £20 million into the bird-brained venture, and . . . lost everything.
- *Precious metals*: gold and silver have been used as currency around the world for centuries. Indeed, so limited are the supplies, that the purchasing power of gold today is roughly the same as it was in the seventeenth century. Thus, some people buy gold and silver as a hedge against inflation. But the fact is that periods of dramatic inflation are rare, and the cost of acquiring, insuring and storing gold and silver is high. In the end, precious metals are not a great investment. Buy them only if you like to wear them.

If you love a particular type of collectible, then enjoy it as a hobby. But prices for collectibles rise and fall as fads emerge and vanish unpredictably. Invest your 'play-money' only, and don't bet your future on collectibles.

HOW MUCH RISK AM I COMFORTABLE WITH?

In general, risk and reward go hand in hand: the greater the risk, the greater the potential return from an investment; the lower the risk, the lower the return. The trick is to find the balance between risk and reward that is right for you. (Please consult the Risk Spectrum chart on page 173.)

Five Time-tested Investment Strategies

1) *Buy and Hold:*
- High-quality, undervalued companies
- Dividend reinvestment
- Stock splits

2) *Instalment Investing (Cost Averaging):*
(Mostly used with unit trusts, but can be used with individual stocks)
- Invest a fixed amount at regular intervals in a unit trust or in company shares

3) *Indexed Investing:*
- Use 'tracker funds' as your core portfolio
- Perhaps invest a small percentage of your money in individual stocks

4) *Recapture your initial investment and let your profits ride:*
- This is really a practical approach to the preceding strategies. Once your securities have increased in value, sell off enough of them to recapture the money you initially invested (plus any interest it may have earned in a building society account). Then let your profits continue to work for you. If the market declines then you are no worse off than if you had saved the money from the beginning and never taken the risk.

5) *The 'Dart Board' Approach:*
- Some people believe that there is no predictable pattern of price movement, so that investments picked by throwing a dart blindly at a list of stocks will perform just as well as those that are carefully chosen by investment professionals. Here's how the darts average

against the experts in the *Wall Street Journal*'s on-going series of investment contests:

	Experts	Darts
Win/lose	67 per cent	33 per cent
Average investment performance	42 per cent	37 per cent

(This measures the performance of all securities selected by both the experts and the dartboard for an average six-month period since the inception of the contest.)

In this contest, at least, the experts clearly beat the dart board.

In this century, relatively risky investments, such as stocks, have resulted in returns of about 10 per cent per year; safer investments, in such things as bonds (some 5 per cent) and savings accounts (about 4 per cent), have had correspondingly lesser returns. But it comes as no surprise that high-risk investments often result in high rates of failure. The risk of stocks, of course, is that they are subject to short-term fluctuations in value. Thus, in order to earn the generous returns you always hear about, you need to have a stomach for volatility and be willing to invest for the long term. Over the next year or two, the stocks you buy may rise or fall in value; over the next twenty years, however, they're almost sure to rise.

It's safe to say that no one should put all of their money in the stock market, and no one should invest their emergency fund or money that they will certainly need in the short term. All investments are risky, and some are more so than others.

Contrary to the popular misconception, however, there is a big difference between saving (which implies no risk) and investing (which implies a reasonable degree of risk). And there is a big difference between investing and gambling (which implies a short-term, highly risky pursuit of profits). Although investing can be risky, it is definitely *not* the same as blowing £10,000 on roulette or having a flutter on a horse in the Grand National. Gambling – whether in cards, on sporting events, or in the stock-market – is a losing proposition in the long term. (That's why the casino owners can afford to build their grand *palazzos* in Las Vegas and Monte Carlo: the losses at the tables go straight into the owners' pockets.)

What is the extent of your risk tolerance? The telling indicator is sleepless nights and obsessive days.

I have a colleague at work who constantly invests his money, and constantly checks the stock prices on his computer. He'll tell you he's just 'curious' to see how his portfolio is doing, but he's clearly agitated. Indeed, any time there is a hint of any drop in stock prices, he *sprints* to the computer to check. If it's true, and the market is down, he starts worrying about selling off all of his holdings. This is an over-reaction – and a clear indication that he is over-invested, in both monetary and psychological terms. In other words, he's operating beyond his risk tolerance. And his fretful days are surely followed by sleepless nights.

Another friend has a very disciplined approach to investing. Like me, she came from a poor background, and she invests only in blue-chip stock for the long term. Further, she only invests the 'extra' money she'd 'waste' on things such as clothes and shoes, and only allows herself to check her accounts once a month. 'When I invest money I pretend I've lost it and it's gone,' she says. 'Having been so poor, it's emotionally hard for me to let go of my money, but intellectually I know this is the best way to prepare for my future.' She knows her risk tolerance, has clear investment goals, and sticks to her plan resolutely. Her eyes, she says, 'are on the prize'.

Understanding your tolerance for financial risk and learning to set realistic investment goals isn't easy. Novice investors are cautioned to think in terms of building wealth over the long term, rather than to speculate wildly for short-term profits. But your investing goals will not remain static: as your financial status changes, and you become a more sophisticated investor, you may adjust your objectives and fine-tune the kinds of securities you hold.

WHAT IS MY INVESTMENT GOAL?

When my friend Nigel says his investment goal is to make his money 'work' for him, he's being far too vague. If he is to have a reasonable chance of achieving his dreams, he needs to state more clearly what his investment goals are. This is important for you, too, because you will use the statement of your goals both as a guide to the right types of investments for you and as a benchmark against which to measure the performance of your investments.

Of course, the ways people with similar financial profiles choose to invest their money are as varied as their fingerprints. A person whose goal is to generate income he can use in the near future might want to purchase stocks that pay high dividends. A person whose goal is to build up money for retirement twenty or more years in the future, on the other hand, may invest in stocks with longer-term potential. A third person may have some extra 'fun' money and decide to speculate on stocks the prices of which fluctuate widely in the short term, in the hope that she will make a small profit.

To help you decide which investing profile best suits you, here are the four most common investment goals:

Conservative growth (also known as 'wealth building')

This is your goal if you are investing for the long term – for retirement twenty or more years in the future, for example. The conservative growth investor is concerned with accumulating a large amount of wealth over a long period of time, and is ready to set aside small amounts every month and let them grow untouched. The conservative growth investor doesn't worry about short-term fluctuations in price, since she doesn't need to cash in the investment any time soon; and she doesn't need to buy high-risk, fast-growth shares, since she has time to allow the magic of compounding to work on her investments.

Aggressive growth

This is your goal if you are investing for significant medium term gains. The aggressive growth investor is looking for young companies in hot new areas like high-tech, Internet and bio-technology. He or she hopes to find company shares that will grow strongly each year as the company's turnover, or sales, increase. Such a strategy is moderate to high risk: the share prices of such companies fluctuate wildly if performance does not meet expectations. Aggressive growth investors tend to hold their stock for reasonably long periods of time – as long as earnings and turnover contrive to increase according to expectations.

Income

This is your goal if it's more important to you to receive regular income from your investments than to see them grow for the future. Older investors who are ready for retirement and need funds to pay their monthly bills are often income-oriented, for example. There are particular types of investments that are particularly appropriate for income investors, such as utility stocks, which usually pay regular high dividends to shareholders.

Speculation

This is your goal if you are investing for very high, very short-term returns. Speculation is like gambling, in that possible huge pay-offs – like jackpots at the casino – are overbalanced by the likelihood of losing everything. As with aggressive growth – only more so – few people should focus on speculation. But experienced, knowledgeable investors who are prepared to cope with the ups and downs of roller-coaster markets may want to play at speculation with a few pounds they can afford to lose – they probably will!

RISK CONTROL

Of course, an investor's dream would be to enjoy large returns with little or no risk: this is the investment equivalent of perpetual motion, or the formula for turning rocks into gold – and is equally unattainable. Experience shows that, in virtually every situation, risk and potential rewards rise and fall together. However, investment experts have devised strategies for *controlling* risk, some of which make it possible to increase your potential gains without accepting undue risk.

The most basic way to limit risk in your investments is to spread your money into different kinds of investments. This is known as *Diversification*. What it really means is that rather than putting all of your eggs in one basket, you should spread them around. To protect yourself within a given class of investment, such as stocks, you must diversify by investing in different types of stocks that perform well in changing economic conditions.

Suppose you've invested all your money in shares of a computer company or group of computer companies; if tomorrow's headlines trumpet the invention of a new type of computer from another company that makes all other computers obsolete, your investment may plummet – taking your retirement plans with it. But if you'd invested only 15 per cent of your money in the computer industry, with the rest of your money in cars, food, banking, and other businesses, it's unlikely they would all fall (or rise) together. So even shocking losses in one investment will probably be offset by gains in the others – leaving your investment portfolio in overall good shape.

WHAT IS THE RIGHT MIX OF INVESTMENTS?

Too often, people cobble together their investments in a haphazard way, and give little thought to how a well planned mix of investments can minimise their risks and optimise their chances of achieving their investing goals. This needn't be the case. The systematic placement of money into various classes of investments, such as stocks, bonds, smaller companies, precious metals, collectibles, or the international markets, for example, is known as *Asset Allocation*.

Successful asset allocation reduces the risk of a gyrating market (when one investment is down in value, the others are hopefully moving up), but it requires the analysis of a good deal of information. This isn't easy to do. Furthermore, there is neither a perfect way of assessing investments nor a common approach to finding the best mix of assets for all investors.

A seasoned investment professional can advise you on strategy, but one rule of thumb is the static or 'robot' asset allocation mix: it consists of putting 55 per cent of your money into stocks, 35 per cent into bonds, and 10 per cent into 'cash' equivalents (meaning money you have instant access to). This kind of mix keeps you diversified: most of your money is in investments that have historically shown the highest returns, while some of it is in safer harbours – just to be sure you are prepared for the worst.

Another theory used by financial advisers recommends that

your total investment in stocks should be equal to 100 per cent minus your age: thus, if you are thirty-five years old, 65 per cent of your investment assets should be in stocks. Using this model, your investment portfolio will become more conservative as you age because the amount you have invested in stocks will decline over time.

THE DOG'S *DERRIÈRE*, OR, WHY I SHOULD NEVER HAVE INVESTED IN RUMOURS

When you buy a stock based on a rumour, consider where you stand on the rumour food-chain: you are probably not on the A-list, with Prince William, or the B-list, with Posh Spice, or even the C-list, with some has-been footballer. No, you (like most of us) are almost certainly on the D-list. That would be D for dog – or, as my grandmother used to say, 'You're the thing the dog sits on when it's a cold day.' A dog's *derrière*: is that where you want your investing advice to come from?

I learned about investing on rumours the way I usually learn my most valuable lessons – the hard way.

In 1985, the US healthcare system was rapidly changing, and a friend of a friend/stockbroker recommended I buy shares in a healthcare company that he promised was going to 'change the world'. Having never heard of the company, or invested in stock before, I felt complimented when this sophisticated investment professional gave me an 'inside tip' about this 'great' opportunity. Immediately I began to fantasise about how much money I was going to make, my new Fifth Avenue apartment with a view over Central Park, the servants who would peel my grapes . . . Doing no homework at all, I marched out and basically threw my wallet at that company. I was just too pleased with myself. A few months later the stock began to tumble. My new 'friend' the

The Risk Spectrum

There is a big difference in the degree of risk associated with these financial products – from vehicles for saving (which implies no risk) to investing cautiously (which implies buying securities for the long term, with a reasonable degree of risk), to outright speculating (which implies short-term, highly risky pursuit of profits:

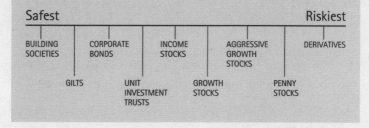

stockbroker advised me to bail out quickly. And so I did, like a rat scurrying from a sinking ship. I lost more money than I care to talk about, even to this day. So much for the rumour mill.

Without doubt, I lack a certain objectivity when it comes to healthcare stocks. I have a tendency to be a wee bit hypochondriacal – the idea of germs can sometimes make me nervous, so just imagine how I react to illness or death. And so, as I scurried away from my sinking healthcare investment, I was probably scurrying away from images of my own sickness and decay – or so my psychologist might have said. Now that I know myself as an investor, I avoid healthcare stocks like the plague.

In a way, I was lucky. I learned a valuable lesson on my very first stock trade, a lesson I have never forgotten: do your own homework before you buy a stock, and know yourself as an investor. I should have looked up information about the company's products, services and management, and charts of its stock prices.

Then I learned a second lesson. The stock I had just sold at a substantial loss began to recover, and after a few years that company has managed to do quite well – although it hasn't exactly 'changed the world'. If I had patiently held on to that stock, and invested for the long term, I would have made a handsome profit.

But wisdom exists in retrospect, and opportunities exist over the horizon. I could have let this negative experience sour me on the stock market for ever; instead, I used it as a learning opportunity. Because I started investing late in life, I knew I had to take some risks: as time went on, I began to get the hang of it. Today, I still make mistakes when I invest, but I make fewer of them. When I look back on my career, I can recall each and every penny I've lost; but I also think about how much better my life is for the risks I've been willing to take. Investing in stocks is risky, but so was leaving home to go out into the world.

How to Buy a Stock

Let's imagine that this chapter has inspired in you the desire to invest in stocks. How do you get started?

Step 1: pick a company to invest in. As a novice investor, don't expect to go to a stockbroker and have him or her recommend a share to you that is going to bring you instant riches. You have to bring with you some ideas about a company or types of companies in which you want to invest. If you don't have specific investment ideas, then take a deep breath and cool down. Use your enthusiasm to begin investigating companies that are potential investments. These companies could be businesses that you use or interact with each day, such as the telephone company, the maker of your mobile phone, the supermarket, a computer maker, a software company or your Internet provider.

Step 2: research the company in detail. A publication called *Company Refs* is a great place to get objective, third-party analysis of a company's possible future performance. (This publication is available at many public libraries and is updated periodically.) More and more information is being made available via the Internet. At any of the shareholder conferences held periodically in large cities throughout the UK, many of these Internet-based information services companies provide lots of free information about their services.

Step 3: place your order. Now that you have selected the share you wish to buy, you can place your order through your local bank, through an advisory broker, or through an execution only broker. In addition to the investment advice that your receive, the major difference between these is the commission, with the execution only broker charging the lowest. When you place your order, you must specify whether you want the value of your trade to include commissions (dealing costs) or you want these to be added to the total value of your purchase. Commission and dealing cost in the UK should begin to drop as on-line investing becomes much more widely available.

Step 4: your final decision involves how you want your securities to be held. Do you want to get the stock certificate yourself or do you want the securities to be held in nominee name (i.e., the name of the brokerage firm)?

Now that you have bought some shares, the next question that quickly pops up in people's minds is, 'When do I sell?' Unfortunately, no perfect sell (or buy) signal exists. You can set a target price – both above and below your purchase price – at which you will sell the stock. You can also decide to hold the shares for as long as you believe there is reasonable likelihood that the price will continue to appreciate. Whichever method you choose, don't feel that you have to stick to it for ever.

CHAPTER 8

PROTECT WHAT YOU HAVE: THE IMPORTANCE OF INSURANCE, WILLS AND PENSIONS

The Alvin Hall Quick Quiz on Saving Your Assets

- Do you assume that you will always have a steady job and good health, and that insurance is not worth paying for?
- Do you expect the government to cover all of your health and welfare costs into your dotage?
- If you are self-employed, do you think it costs too much to buy even the most basic insurance policy?
- Do you have children and other relatives who rely on your income, but you have no life assurance?
- Do you have a family (or dependants) and own property, but no will?
- Do you think you are too young, or too old, to start contributing to a pension scheme?

If you answered Yes to four or more of these questions, then you are in need of a reality check. For a primer on protecting your family and yourself against life's unexpected surprises, read on.

'*You* are all you will ever have,' my grandmother used to caution, 'so protect what you have.'

It was good advice, and hard won, and it has forced me to ask myself: if something happens to me, who will I turn to? I am a single man, and my own bread-winner, and I have come to realise that I have to look out for myself. But I didn't always think this way. Like many people, I used to suffer from the White Knight syndrome.

For years, I believed subconsciously that if I ever ran into deep trouble, my friends would help bail me out. Then I moved to New York City, and began to work at a friend's company: I had been promised equity (part ownership) in the firm, and so was willing to make sacrifices; I trusted that if I worked hard, and held up my end of the bargain, I would be taken care of. And for a while I was. Four and a half years later, however, the company was sold and I received nothing. It was a disheartening experience, to say the least, and it left me feeling naïve and vulnerable. And that's when it first dawned on me that I could never again rely on others to look out for my best interests.

I was lucky to have this experience early enough in my career that I was still employable. I dusted myself off, and got on with life a bit wiser. With time, I was able to weave my own safety net: I bought disability insurance, health insurance and some life insurance; I had a proper will drawn up; and I managed to save a year's worth of income in the bank. My goal was to become completely self-sufficient.

Most people don't like to think about bad things happening to them, because 'bad things don't happen to good people'. But we all know tragic stories: some people learn from others' experiences, while others remain in denial that bad things can happen to them, too.

In today's fast-changing society, where old industries are downsizing or imploding, and new ones are sprouting up at a breakneck pace, you would do well to take the modest steps outlined below to protect yourself, your family and your possessions from life's unexpected surprises.

SAFEGUARD YOUR ASSETS

As Britain's traditional Welfare State changes, private insurance is becoming an increasingly important part of everyone's financial planning. In the future, the State may no longer provide the cradle-to-grave health and benefits system so many have relied on in the past. Indeed, even now the protection guaranteed by the State is hardly comprehensive.

If you are faced with a flood, a car wreck, a sudden injury, or any other unpredictable loss, the last thing you want to think about is how your bad luck could turn even worse – by bankrupting you and your loved ones. While there are hundreds of insurance policies available to protect you and your family, they are not cheap, and you certainly don't need them all.

What *do* you need? While no one insurance policy can cover you for every possible crisis, you should consider the following forms of financial self-defence.

Health insurance
Everyone needs health insurance, no matter how healthy, wealthy, wise, or hypochondriacal. If your employer covers you, consider yourself fortunate: although you may have to

contribute part of the cost, the cost will be much less than purchasing your own insurance. But don't take company insurance for granted: tedious as it may seem, it is well worth your while to go over the fine print and find out exactly what kind of coverage you are granted through your work. Then take steps to plug any holes on your own.

Generally, the amount you will pay for insurance coverage depends on your age, the state of your health, and the level of cover you choose. There are three main types of insurance for when you become ill:

Income Protection: if you suffer an accident or become ill and cannot work, this plan will pay you up to 65 per cent of your before tax income until you return to work, die, or reach the age at which you have decided your benefits should stop (which could be your normal age of retirement).

Three types of cover are available: *Own occupation* (when you cannot continue to work in your regular occupation and are not working in any other), *Any suitable occupation* (when you cannot work in any job you are qualified for) and *Any occupation* (when you cannot return to any kind of job at all).

If you work for yourself, you should look into this scheme because if things go wrong you won't have an employer offering sick-pay. But there are drawbacks: this kind of insurance can be expensive, and you can't claim a pay-out immediately. (The deferred periods are normally for four, thirteen, twenty-six or fifty-two weeks.)

Critical illness insurance: if you are diagnosed with a specified illness, such as multiple sclerosis, stroke, heart attack or cancer, among others, critical illness coverage will pay out a cash lump sum. You can use this money as you like – for nursing care, say, if you are unable to care for yourself, or even to pay off your mortgage.

Two types of cover are available: *term* cover (which insures you for a designated number of years, called the term), and *whole-life* cover (which insures you for your entire life). It's cheaper for couples to take out joint cover.

One drawback is that you won't get cover for certain kinds of cancer, HIV or AIDS; and this insurance can be costly.

Private medical insurance (PMI): this will pay the cost of private or specialised medical care when you become ill. Three types of cover are available: top-level, medium-level, budget-level. If you are satisfied with your care by the National Health Service, PMI is not essential. But with NHS waiting lists currently running up to eighteen months for non-urgent operations, many people are looking to Private Medical Insurance in order to jump the queue. If you want quick access to a specialist and plush hospital accommodation, then this insurance is for you.

Long-term care insurance

In the old days, you could expect the State to help you with long-term nursing care costs. But now people with assets worth over £16,000 (generally including the property they own) have had to pay their own way into old age. Residential home and nursing care costs are quite high – full-time residential care costs an average of £13,260 per year, while average nursing home fees are £18,720 per year, but can be as much as £30,000 – and so the question of who should be responsible for long-term care has been the subject of much debate.

The Royal Commission on Long-Term Care report was published in March 1999 and proposed that the costs be shared by the State and individuals in an equitable, transparent way. The commission held that long-term care should be split between living costs, housing costs and personal care: personal care would be paid for by the government, while the rest would be means tested. The commission report arguably raises as many questions as it answers, and whatever the final decisions are, they will take years to implement. What is clear, however, is that there is a move towards getting people to fund their own long-term care.

In the meantime, insurance companies have developed long-term care insurance to fill the gap between what the State will provide and what you will have to pay. The maximum benefit depends on how much you are insured for, but usually tops out at £36,000 a year. The policy takes effect if it is assessed that you cannot look after yourself on a daily basis. This is determined by an Activities of Daily Living (ADL) list, which varies slightly from insurer to insurer, to ensure that your sustenance, mobility and hygiene are adequate.

Life assurance

When you die life assurance protects the people who rely on your income. If you have a family, this is particularly important. Fortunately, for most people, an adequate level of life assurance coverage is quite affordable.

The rule of thumb on life assurance is: if you are single, and without dependants, you don't need it; if you are married without children, and your spouse can handle the basic living expenses on her/his own, you don't need it; if you have kids, or any other financial dependants, however, you definitely need it.

Even if your employer gives you some life assurance benefits (if you die in service), or your mortgage is backed by an endowment policy (which pays a specific amount upon death), it may not be adequate to support your family in your absence. There are a wide range of policies and ways to mix and match them, and it is worth comparing prices and benefits to get the best package.

The cheapest and simplest way to ensure you have adequate coverage is to take out *term* assurance – a life coverage that lasts for a designated term of, say, twenty years, with a fixed payout, say £500,000. There are several kinds of term assurance, and the kind that suits you depends on your circumstances.

One way to work out the amount of coverage you need is to multiply your annual income by twenty: so, if you earn £35,000 a year, you will need £700,000 of coverage.

Other kinds of insurance

Once you have insured yourself and your family, it is essential to protect your other assets. Here are some common types of insurance to consider:

Home insurance

Chances are that your house will not be picked up in Kansas and whirled by winds to Oz, like Dorothy's was. But storms are a fact of life – even the rare destructive hurricane, like the storm of 1987 that felled trees and damaged houses across the south-east of England. And in the event of such a calamity, chances are good that even if you click the heels of your ruby slippers three times, your house won't be magically repaired, either. That's why it is important to consider buying home insurance.

There are two types of coverage – *building* insurance, which covers the amount it would cost to rebuild your home and other buildings, as well as the cost of temporary accommodation while your home is being repaired, and *contents* insurance which covers the replacement of possessions in your home. It is important to shop around for the best rates in this fiercely competitive market, and to understand completely what is covered in the policy you decide on.

Motor insurance

By law you must have motor insurance on your car – and with absent-minded drivers like me and my friends on the road, that's a good thing. An accident is not always your fault, after all. One friend was driving recently, saw the light turn red as he approached an intersection, but didn't slow down; after he crashed into the back of the car in front of him, he said, he 'couldn't remember what red meant'. (This is a true story.) Luckily, both drivers were uninjured and insured.

Basic policies cover any damage or injury you may cause while driving; more comprehensive policies cover a lot more, although you have to pay more for them. If you make no claims on your policy, your premium will be reduced over time and you will be entitled to a No Claims Bonus. Again, this is a sharply competitive arena, so shop around for the best rates.

Accident, sickness and redundancy insurance
This coverage has become increasingly popular in the UK, as a bulwark against the wave of redundancies. It is designed to protect your significant monthly debts – such as mortgage, car loan, or credit card payments – should you be laid off or become incapacitated. The cover is usually limited to a year, and it can be costly. However, you may want to consider this type of insurance if it can mean the difference between your family having to move to a cheaper home or being able to stay put should your income cease for any reason.

GOOD WILL HUNTING

'Where there's a will there are relatives,' goes the old Yiddish saying. My version of this same thought is: 'Where there is *no* will, there is bound to be a fight.'

You probably don't plan to die tomorrow, and the very thought of a will may depress you, but if you want to ensure that your hard-earned money and much-loved possessions are handled in the way you want, a tamper-proof will is essential. This is particularly true if you are the primary breadwinner in the family, or if you are in a relationship that is not approved of by your family.

The importance of having a proper will was made starkly clear to me a few years ago when a friend, a member of a gay couple, died 'intestate' – without a will. His parents, who had always disapproved of the relationship, seized all of the possessions and property that the couple had accumulated together over a decade. The surviving partner was left both bereaved *and* bereft.

While you can save on lawyers' fees by buying a standard will from a stationery shop, this is not a DIY situation. A will can be legally challenged after your death, on many different counts, and it is essential that everything is in order and the legal language is properly used. To get your will right, it is worth the time and money to have it drawn up professionally.

If you die 'intestate' – without a will – there are some basic rules on what happens to your property. Below are the rules for England and Wales. Northern Ireland has virtually the same rules (although in Northern Ireland married people under eighteen can make a will, while that is not the case in England and Wales). Scotland has its own set of rules.

I include these rules in part to show that you really need to take this process into your own hands and make up a will that distributes your property in a way that will satisfy *you* rather than the Crown. Dividing up an estate is a complex process, which can take years. Unmarrieds take special note:

- If you are married and have no other living relatives, your spouse will inherit the whole estate.
- If you are married without children, but have parents and siblings, your spouse will get the first £200,000 of your estate, personal possessions and half of the rest. The other half goes to your parents, and if they are not alive the estate is divided between your brothers and sisters.

- If you are married with children, your spouse inherits personal possessions, the first £125,000, and the income from half of the remainder for life. The other half is inherited by the children.
- If you have divorced, your ex-partner does not get a share of the estate if you die without a will. Any children you've had with an ex-partner have a full claim, however.
- If you live with a partner but are not married, the law does not automatically recognise your partner's claim. He or she will have to apply to the Crown administrator for a share of the estate. Any children you've had together have the full claim, whether they were born inside or outside marriage.
- If you have no living relatives, your estate will pass into the hands of the Crown. Anyone who thinks they have a claim on your estate can apply for their share.

In Scotland, the rules are slightly different. If you die intestate in Scotland, your spouse gets a right to your house up to a value of £110,000, its furnishings up to a value of £20,000, and cash up to £30,000 (£50,000 if you have no children). Your spouse also gets a percentage of everything valued above this. Your children get everything else.

While it's possible for your children to get nothing if you die without a will in Scotland, it's not possible to exclude your spouse or children from your will. Unlike in England, marriage does not automatically invalidate any previous will.

Do these rules strike you as arcane, confusing, and a little arbitrary? Good – that's exactly what they are. I've detailed them here to bring home to you how badly your wishes and dreams for the future may be distorted if you die intestate.

Just one example: if you're married with small children and you die, you might assume your spouse will be able to handle your assets as he or she sees fit. But that won't be true if you have no will. Indeed, a sizeable chunk of the money may be tied up in trust, greatly reducing your spouse's freedom to look after the children or to buy a new home, for example. Don't leave your loved ones' future at the mercy of the estate lawyers. Have a will drawn up that reflects *your* wishes accurately.

PLAN YOUR RETIREMENT

Everybody dreams of the joys of a comfortable retirement – except me. I'm too busy to retire, and I'll probably drop dead while stuck on the phone or in a meeting.

You, on the other hand, are probably already planning a sun-splashed and wine-drenched retirement in Provence. But before you accept that gold wristwatch for good service and pack your *espadrilles*, make sure you've read the minutiae of your pension scheme – or you may suffer the fate of my friend Mabel.

Mabel and Harry were happily married for decades, but they rarely talked about their joint finances. He gave her money to run the house, but otherwise took care of their accounts. Once in a while, she'd pluck up her courage and ask him about their pension scheme. 'It's all taken care of, love,' he'd answer. 'I've got a terrific pension through my job, and there's nothing to worry about.' Then, one morning not long after Harry had retired, Mabel was in the kitchen and heard a noise: she turned, and found him face-first in his oatmeal, dead from a heart-attack. Later, she was further traumatised when she discovered that while there was a little bit of money in their savings account, the pension Harry had arranged was a 'single-life pension'. For years single-life pensions were a very popular investment because they promised to pay the highest premium. People focused on the money they'd be receiving upon retirement, not on the fact that such a plan covers only one person. Indeed, once Harry died all the money in his pension reverted to the company. At age sixty-three, Mabel had virtually nothing to live on, and had to go back to work at a chemist's, where she continues to work today.

You can never be too young or too old, too rich or too poor to start planning your retirement. As soon as you can afford to start putting something in a pension scheme – even if it's only £10 a month – you should do so on a regular basis. There are many advantages to this kind of saving:

- You're not taxed on the income you contribute to a pension scheme.
- The longer your contributions have to grow the greater your wealth will become. Don't forget about the power of compounding, which we discussed in Chapter 4.
- Pension schemes offer a lot more than just retirement income, they also offer a tax-free lump sum upon retirement, and can include built-in life assurance and pension benefits to your spouse and children.

The government is currently proposing to introduce a new type of pension arrangement, known as a *Stakeholder pension*. These pensions are designed to be more flexible, more easily accessible and to have lower charges than existing personal pension arrangements. Stakeholder pensions will be provided by insurance companies, and all employers will have to offer their employees participation in such a scheme (not all employees will have to contribute, though). The new Stakeholder arrangements are targeted to come into use in April 2001 (see page 193 for details).

So how do you go about setting up a pension scheme?

Pension Contributions as a Percentage of Current Earnings

The longer you wait to begin contributing to a pension scheme, the more onerous your contributions will become, as this chart demonstrates.

Age at which working adults start pension contributions:	Percentage of current salary you must contribute (assuming you plan to retire at age sixty-five):
30 years	13 per cent
40 years	18 per cent
50 years	28 per cent

(*Source*: NatWest)

Work out a budget

The first step is to work out a retirement budget – the expenses you expect to incur each month after you stop working. This will give you a benchmark against which to gauge your existing arrangements, and allow you to make adjustments as you go along. You will need to estimate for both fixed, essential monthly expenses and non-essentials such as holidays, hobbies and the hairdressers, which may be different from the kinds of expenses you have today.

(Please see 'How to Estimate Your Retirement Budget', opposite).

While the best you can hope for is a rough estimate, this budget will give you some general idea of what you need to put away. One factor you must bear in mind is the cost of inflation, which can eat away at your buying power over time. A second factor to bear in mind is that you may live a lot longer than you might think.

Pension Basics: How to Estimate Your Retirement Budget

At today's interest rates, if you'd like to receive £15,000 annual income on retirement at age sixty-five:
aged 30 – pay £208 per month
aged 40 – pay £400 per month
aged 50 – pay £1025 per month

If you'd like to receive £20,000 annual income on retirement:
aged 30 – pay £277
aged 40 – pay £531
aged 50 – pay £1365

If you'd like to receive £30,000 annual income on retirement:
aged 30 – pay £416
aged 40 – pay £797
aged 50 – £2048

(*Source*: Norwich Union)

Pick a pension scheme

The State pension system has been fiddled with ever since its inception in 1948 because it is so costly to run. Today, State pension payments are small, and may be getting smaller, so don't rely too heavily on them in your planning. The government is continuing to review the system, and it is worth following new developments. If your employer offers a pension scheme you should definitely join it, and if you are self-employed you need to sign up for a personal pension scheme as soon as possible.

Here are the pension basics:

State pensions

The State pension is composed of two parts. The first is known as the *Basic State Pension*: you are entitled to this if you have made sufficient National Insurance contributions during your working life. Its current value is £67.50 per week for individuals and £107.90 per week for couples. The second part of the State pension is the *State Earnings Related Pension Scheme* (SERPS): this currently pays up to a maximum of £125 per week. You can opt out of SERPS, in which case, when it comes to retirement, you will have to purchase an annuity. This is an investment contract with an insurance company, into which you pay either a lump sum or contributions over a number of years. When you reach a certain age, the annuity contract usually begins to make monthly payments to you for the rest of your life.

Employers' pensions

Probably the best way to plan for your retirement is to contribute to your employer's pension scheme. Some experts consider a company pension a 'deferred salary' that you work for now and collect later.

What makes these schemes so valuable is that employers will either pay for the whole scheme or contribute handsomely towards a pension for you. If such a scheme is available to you, it would be foolish not to take advantage of it straight away – even if you don't intend on spending your entire career with that company.

There are two types of company pension. With *Final Salary* schemes, your pension depends on the length of your employment and your salary at retirement. With *Money Purchase* schemes, your pension depends on the amount paid into a pension fund, and how well the fund performs; upon retirement, you use the fund to buy an annuity contract that pays you income for the rest of your life.

Stakeholder pensions

If you are a parent who stays at home to raise children, can you contribute to a pension even though you have no earned income? If you have chosen to stop working temporarily in order to take care of elderly parents or other relatives, can you continue to contribute to a pension scheme that you've already set up? In April 2001, when the Government introduces its new Stakeholder pension scheme, the answer to these questions will thankfully be 'yes'. No longer will you have to have a job or be self-employed in order to contribute to a pension. The Stakeholder pension scheme eliminates this requirement. This new pension scheme is available to all people, whether or not they have earned income.

Individuals can contribute up to £3,600 per year. [NOTE: The Government may increase these amounts periodically to reflect inflation, interest rates, and other factors that affect the value of money.] As with all other pensions, you cannot withdraw any money from the scheme until you retire. All gains earned on the money in this pension scheme are not subject to taxation until they are withdrawn at retirement.

While anyone can set up his or her own Stakeholder pension, the people the Government believes will benefit most from this new scheme are those who earn between £10,000 and £20,000 per year. Because people in this income bracket may not be sufficiently covered by the state pension scheme, they can provide themselves with additional retirement income by setting up individual Stakeholder pensions.

Clearly, every penny earned towards a comfortable retirement is important to all of us – especially to people in the income range cited above. Realising this, the Government has tried to design Stakeholder pensions to be low cost, flexible, and secure. To keep costs (such as management and administrative fees) low, the Government has capped the annual charge on Stakeholder pensions. The maximum charge is set at 1 per cent of the total value of each person's pension. This is substantially less than the average annual fees charged on most pensions in the UK. In practical terms, this means that more of the profits from the investments made via a Stakeholder pension should end up in the pensioners' pockets.

This benefit may, some people believe, be undermined by the quality of the advice provided by investment advisers. These professionals may be reluctant, if not totally indifferent, to provide their 'professional services' at such a low fee. Will the people who need prudent and appropriate financial advice the most be treated improperly? I believe this is a valid concern. However, don't let yourself be immobilised by negativism and fear, and therefore fail to set up a Stakeholder pension for your dotage!

You should view setting up your own Stakeholder pensions as giving you three opportunities:

- To be more pro-active in shaping your financial future (specifically your retirement).
- To educate yourself about specific types of investments (unit trusts, investments trusts, shares) so that you know how to make suitable and prudent decisions for yourself.
- To monitor regularly the performance of your investments and/or your financial adviser to make sure all are on track to help you accomplish your long-term retirement goal.

Stakeholder pensions have special provisions for people who work for small companies (those with five or more employees). If the small company you work for offers no occupational pension scheme, it will now be obligated to offer Stakeholder pensions to all employees. Your employer must offer you the ability to make your contribution via salary deduction. Importantly, company-sponsored Stakeholder pensions schemes must also be registered and approved to ensure that the money invested is handled properly.

A Stakeholder pension's flexibility lies in the fact that you can move it with you when you change jobs. If you are a person like me who changes jobs like Elizabeth Taylor changes husbands, this feature is a real benefit. It should significantly reduce the likelihood of people having what I call, 'lost' pensions – those that you somehow forget about over the years as you move from one job to another. When you take your pension with you to your new job, you can, if you wish, continue to contribute through the same manager or administrator.

It is important to remember that the terms 'secure' and 'risk-free' do not mean the same thing in the world of investments. If the money in your Stakeholder pension is invested in shares, unit trusts, or any other type of securities, then there is always the possibility that the value of the investment may decline. You must be aware of the amount of risk you can tolerate when selecting the types of securities in which your pension money will be invested.

As the launch date of Stakeholder pensions approaches, the Government will release more specific details about the scheme. Be sure to read financial newspapers and magazines to find out other details about the plan. One thing that does seem clear at this point is that everyone should consider opening a Stakeholder pension. After all, we could all use a little extra money to help make our golden years comfortable and fun – whether that means an around-the-world holiday, a rented villa in Tuscany, or a refreshing bit of aesthetic surgery.

Personal pensions

If you work for a small company, or for yourself, you will have to make all contributions to your pension fund yourself. Upon retirement, you can withdraw, tax-free, up to 25 per cent of the value of the fund in a lump sum; you must use the rest to buy an annuity contract to provide you with income for the rest of your life.

Personal pensions offer a great deal of flexibility – you can choose how much to invest, where to invest it and what kind of risk you prefer. These pensions are generally *Unit-linked* schemes (in which benefits depend on the performance of units invested in a fund of shares, gilts or bonds) or *With-profits* schemes (designed to smooth out the peaks and troughs of the stock market by investing in a broad range of securities, cash and also property. Bonuses are added to your policy each year, and they cannot be taken away by the company. Finally, once you have reached retirement, a terminal bonus is paid which boosts your fund).

With all of these schemes, it's important, once you've set up your pension, to continue monitoring how your arrangements are working out. Your life situation, after all, changes. Hopefully, your circumstances improve steadily, and this change (or, indeed, any change) must be reflected in your pension contributions. Perhaps it is the Baptist in me that feels you should 'give 'til it hurts' – only this time, remember you are giving to yourself.

Everybody enjoys the fruits of their labour in their own way. I like to buy clothes, antiques and fine art – but I don't take expensive holidays, entertain lavishly, own a car, or redecorate my house frequently. Indeed, certain friends tell me I need to 'lighten up' and enjoy my success more overtly. But it just isn't me.

As I grow older I become increasingly aware that I need to plan for my Golden Years, when I'll be less active and more frail. Difficult as it is to face, this inevitability is a powerful motivator for me. After all, I know very well what my life could be like if I don't plan ahead: it could be exactly like the impoverished circumstances in which I began life. I am determined never again to be forced to live a subsistence existence. When I think about my drive to prepare myself for senescence, I envision Scarlett O'Hara in *Gone With the Wind*, raising her fist to the sky and declaiming, 'As God is my witness, I'll never go hungry again!'

CHAPTER 9

THE FACTS ON
FINANCIAL ADVISERS

Alvin Hall's Quick Quiz on Financial Advice

- Do you believe that investments should 'take care of themselves'?
- Are you so intimidated by the jargon of financial experts that you avoid asking basic questions?
- Have you signed up with a financial adviser without checking his or her credentials?
- Are you uncertain about how financial professionals are paid?
- Do you assume that the financial advice a broker, banker or accountant gives you is unbiased?
- Have you ever bought an investment like a unit trust or a pension without shopping around?

If you answered 'Yes' to any of the above questions, then you need advice on financial advisers.

M y friend Charlotte recently visited a professional financial adviser whom I'll call Michael. She works freelance and wanted help in choosing a suitable pension. Michael went on at great length about various schemes, and drew a chart that purported to show how the plans worked; he used complicated words to explain the chart's meaning and really seemed to know what he was talking about. But when Charlotte looked at it, all she saw was 'a bunch of squiggly lines'. As Michael wrapped up the session, Charlotte meekly nodded her head and said 'Right,' as if she understood everything. Then she wrote him a cheque for £100, and walked out feeling cowed and mystified. 'He's so smart and I'm so stupid,' she remembers thinking. 'I just don't understand finance.'

Later, when Charlotte showed the chart to me, I didn't understand it either. It *was* just a bunch of squiggly lines – more reminiscent of one of Cy Twombly's scribbly drawings than a useful pension planner. Astonished, I asked Charlotte: 'If you didn't understand what Michael was saying, why didn't you ask him to explain it better?'

She sighed, and answered: 'It would have been, you know, awkward. Besides, it all seemed to make perfect sense to him.'

'But you're *paying* him for advice and you're entitled to understand the information he's charging you for,' I said. 'If he ends up losing your money, and you complain, he'll simply say, "If you didn't understand what I said you should have asked the question." '

Have you ever found yourself in Charlotte's position? Are you intimidated by the gnostic symbols and inscrutable financial-speak of the 'experts'? Do you find yourself spellbound by money, or trembling in fear and incomprehension at the learned Druids of the City who seem to have occult powers beyond the ken of mere mortals like you? If so, you are not alone.

It isn't easy to find good financial advice. There are many reasons for this. One is that finance *can* be a complex topic, although it needn't be handled like nuclear physics. Another is the age-old tendency of experts in any field to use exclusive jargon, which can intimidate the uninitiated. Sadly, the financial world has its share of such self-anointed gurus. Finally, there's the fact that the industry has been undergoing a wrenching transition. Before July 1997, financial advisers did not require any professional training at all: the result was a lack of uniformity and many innocent investors were duped into buying unsuitable insurance or pension schemes, which paid the sales people huge commissions. In the wake of these scandals, many people remain understandably sceptical of financial advisers.

While hiring a competent, ethical financial adviser can help you make informed choices, you must remember that there is no such thing as free advice. Indeed, many advisers work on commission. Whatever name they go by – broker, adviser, counsellor – they are salespeople, first and foremost, and are therefore unlikely to suggest a strategy or product that has no payoff for them. If you are interviewing a financial adviser with the notion of having him or her to help manage your portfolio, then you must always ask yourself: will this person benefit financially if I follow his or her advice? If so, consider it sceptically.

There are good reasons to hire someone to help you do things you are not interested in, or able to do, yourself: if you want a professionally-drawn-up will, for example, or dislike crunching numbers, or are leery of the stock market, then a professional adviser can save you time and money.

Indeed, some people are surprised to learn that I use a stockbroker. Why, they wonder, does someone who spends most of his waking hours (and occasional sleepless nights) thinking about Wall Street need a broker? The answer is simple: I am often so busy that I cannot spend the time to do the research my portfolio requires; my broker, on the other hand, researches stocks for a living and gives me good tips.

It's up to me whether or not I take my broker's advice, of course – and often I don't. Some of her more outlandish suggestions cause me to burst out laughing, while other ideas simply don't interest me, are in industries that I don't like, or are too risky for my tastes. My broker is not my sole source of investment information, and I often know enough about a company, or market sector, to make an informed decision on my own. But the fact is, she has occasionally brought a good suggestion to the table that I was unaware of – such as the time a few years ago when she recommended I buy shares of Pfizer, the pharmaceutical company. As you know by now, I tend to shy away from medical-related stocks for hypochondriacal reasons. Thankfully, my broker wore down my resistance and convinced me that Pfizer was going to perform well over time – and with the 1998 introduction of Viagra, the impotence remedy, it struck pure platinum.

A good adviser can help you put your financial house in order. In return for a fee, he or she should help you:

- assess your past and current financial status
- set realistic financial goals for the future
- recommend a number of strategies to achieve your goals
- help you research and buy good, commission-free products

- help you and your partner or family make important financial decisions
- prioritise your financial tasks.

In the process of working with the adviser, you should learn how to reduce your spending and costs, increase your savings and investment returns, and prepare yourself for both good and bad times in the future.

Financial advisers, of course, are not for everybody. In general, British people rely on financial advisers more than Americans do. But some DIYers dislike taking advice, or (believe it or not) actually enjoy doing their own research and calculations. If you are inclined to do it your own way, then give it a go and create your own plan. If you are stymied, you can always turn to a professional for a second opinion later.

This chapter is, at root, about empowerment: about how to work with competent financial professionals, or devise your own plan competently so that *you* are ultimately in charge of your money, and thus your life.

TYPES OF FINANCIAL ADVISERS

You may not be aware that there are, in fact, three types of professional financial adviser: Independent Financial Advisers, Tied Agents and professionals (such as solicitors and accountants) who give advice as a sideline.

Independent Financial Advisers (IFAs)

The largest group, independent financial advisers, are required by law to give you the best, unbiased advice available. The IFA's job is to carefully review your current financial status, recommend a plan of action and suggest the best financial products for you. While they are generally paid by the hour, or with a flat fee,

What to Expect When Meeting a Financial Adviser

Make sure the adviser:

- Tells you whether they are independent or tied to a specific company.
- Asks you in detail about you and your finances, and your present and future needs. (This is usually called a 'fact find'.)
- Explains why the product is suitable for you and gives you this explanation in writing.
- Gives you a 'Key Features' document that explains vital details such as:
  - the commission and other charges you will have to pay
  - the level of risk
  - the aims and benefits of the product
  (If the product is not covered by the rules, you will not get a Key Features document, but you should still ask for these details.)
- Tells you how long you have to change your mind once you've signed up. This is known as a 'cooling-off period'. Not all products have cooling-off periods, so check.

(*Source*: Financial Services Authority)

some IFAs give their advice free and are paid a commission by the companies whose products they recommend – although they are not 'tied' to these companies (see below).

Most IFAs specialise. For example, some are experts in the stock market, while others know all about insurance and still others track real estate. It is unlikely that one individual can know everything about all of the many financial products available. And so, if you are working with an independent IFA, be sure that he or she knows about the products you are specifically interested in. The alternative is to work with a number of IFAs with different strengths, or go to a large IFA firm, which has specialists in all the areas you need.

You should be absolutely clear about what charges to expect. Since most IFAs are paid by commission, if you don't buy the products they recommend you don't pay them anything. If you do buy an investment on which a commission is charged, be sure you know how much you're paying and when. Consider the impact of the commission when deciding whether or not an investment is right for you.

Before you hire an IFA, be sure to check their references and try to learn enough so that you can spot incompetence early. For more information, call IFA Promotion on 0117 971 1177.

Tied Agents

These advisers are said to be 'tied' because they represent just one firm and its products, and must act on its behalf. While they sometimes call themselves 'financial consultants', to appear objective, these agents are really just salespeople for one company. While they are required to advise you about the most suitable product from their company, if the company they are tied to doesn't have a suitable product then you are not likely to be educated about the very best ways to use your money.

Indeed, Tied Agents are more likely to try to sell you a flash insurance policy (with a steep commission), for instance, than advise you to put your money into your employer's pension scheme (whose costs are low).

Some insurance companies only sell their products through IFAs, but by far the majority of banks, building societies and insurance companies have advisers who sell only their company's products. These advisers are required to give you a full accounting of your financial status before attempting to sell you anything. This can be a helpful process, but the pitfall is that they will then put pressure on you to buy their products. If you do your own research, and comparison shop, it's likely you will find better financial products elsewhere.

Since July, 1997, both tied company salespeople and independent financial advisers have been required to pass three exams to qualify for employment. The Financial Planning Certificate (FPC), run by the Chartered Insurance Institute, is the most common qualification. Most financial advisers take these exams and should have passed FPC 1, 2 and 3. Don't be shy about asking.

Some have more advanced qualifications, such as the Advanced Financial Planning Certificate (AFPC) or the Certified Financial Planner certificate (CFP). Those who receive the CFP have to follow strict rules of conduct and renew their application every year. The Institute of Financial Planning (on 0117 930 4434) will supply details about its members who are CFP qualified and offer independent, fee-based advice.

Finally, the Financial Services Authority (FSA), which regulates the way investments are run and sold, keeps a register of everyone authorised to be an IFA or Tied Agent: before agreeing to work with an agent, check with the FSA (on 0845 606 1234) to make sure the agent is properly registered.

Professionals

If you are looking for specialised advice on, for example, investments or tax planning, you might consider a solicitor or accountant who also gives financial advice on the side.

The Association of Solicitor Investment Managers (AIM) has a free directory of firms that offer financial advice (on 01892 870065). Or you can try Solicitors for Financial Advice (SIFA) on 01372 721172.

Chartered accountants must pass the Initial Test of Competence (ITC). You can get a list of firms that are registered to give investment advice through the Practitioner Bureau (on 01908 548026), or look up the District Society of Chartered Accountants in your local *Yellow Pages*.

STOCKBROKERS

A 'brokerage house' is a financial company that acts as a middle man. They handle the purchase and sale of securities on your behalf, manage the flow of dividends and other investment income into your account, maintain financial records for you and otherwise help you navigate the investment markets. A good broker, whom you trust, and who understands your financial needs, can be an invaluable ally. But finding such a broker isn't easy. Some brokers are interested only in earning quick commissions, and will encourage you to buy and sell stocks – sometimes to excess (a practice known as 'churning'). As with any specialist, it is worth taking your time to find the right broker, and then to develop a good working relationship with him or her.

The three main kinds of brokers are:

Execution-only brokers
As the name implies, these brokers simply execute your trades: you call them and place an order to buy or sell shares, and they will do so. With execution-only brokers, all the responsibility for the trade rests squarely on your shoulders; they are not even remotely interested in acting as your financial therapist. They are paid a commission (that is a percentage of the amount you invest), and are the cheapest option, but will not offer you investment advice.

Advisory brokers
These brokers will execute trades *and* offer you as much investment advice as you want – advice you are free to accept

or reject, as you see fit. If you are looking for someone to talk to, advisory brokers offer a great way to get advice. These brokers are paid a commission, and are more expensive than execution-only brokers. But when the market crashes and you find yourself in a sweat, it is nice to talk to someone who has experienced falling markets before and won't panic.

A full-service brokerage house typically has a research depart-ment that follows individual stocks or market sectors (for example, Technology, Communications, Healthcare, etc.). The information they glean is used to estimate the company's growth and earnings potential, and to make recommendations to the firm's clients. If you have a broker, he or she will take both your investment goals and their own research into account when making recommendations to you. The costs of research are factored into the commissions that you will pay when buying or selling securities.

Portfolio managers

This type of professional money manager is only for those who have lots of money, like the Queen, and who want someone else to invest *part* of their assets for them. Basically, you give such an adviser full discretion over your money: initially, you agree on a general investing plan together; but from then on it is up to the portfolio manager to buy or sell whatever securities they like, and you only find out what they've done after the fact. Such advisers are not common in America (where people like to have greater control over the way their hard-earned dollars are spent), but they are quite popular in the UK, especially among those with new money. I'm not sure why this is, exactly, although I suspect it is rooted in the British tendency to mimic royalty, and the assumption that money is somehow vulgar and should be handled by others.

HOW TO GET STARTED

To find a good adviser, try to get a recommendation from someone you trust who has had a good experience. A referral from a professional source you've dealt with, such as a solicitor or accountant, can also be helpful – but, beware that some unethical professionals trade referrals. The caveat is that you should *always* research the financial adviser, and you should *always* shop around to find a good fit. Also, make sure the adviser is authorised by calling the Financial Services Authority (FSA) on 0845 606 1234.

Here are the basic points to keep in mind:

- If you decide you really need professional advice, decide how much you're willing to spend for it. If you can afford a fee, your best bet is a fee-based IFA.
- Always shop around. Talk to more than one adviser, and find out what qualifications and specialities each brings to the table. Make your decision based on which adviser will best serve *your* specific needs.
- Don't sign on with an adviser who makes you feel pressured, intimidated or uncomfortable. If you don't feel able to ask your adviser anything at all – including 'stupid' questions – you won't get your money's worth out of the relationship.

DIY FINANCIAL ADVICE

Like most do-it-yourself projects, doing your own financial planning requires an investment of time, energy and money. Some people I know revel in the 'game' of learning about how the markets work and crunching the numbers to analyse how

Five Questions to Ask the First Time You Meet an Adviser

1) How many companies' products do you recommend, and why only those companies' products?
2) What other options could I consider apart from the products you recommend?
3) What are the pluses and minuses to this investment?
4) How much commission will you get paid for each of these products?
5) How long am I locked in for? Am I committing myself to making regular payments for a long time?

(*Source*: Financial Services Authority)

their securities are performing. Those who handle their own finances solely to save money, on the other hand, tend to focus on getting the job done quickly and with the minimum hassle. Their results are frequently disappointing.

The most difficult part of directing your own finances may be examining your financial history and correcting any mistakes, so that you can start to plan for the future with a relatively clean slate. For some this takes time, but for others it requires only a few hours. If, on the other hand, you think that figuring your own money history is going to be too complicated, you have nothing to lose by getting a free review from a professional financial adviser: remember, you won't have to pay for a thing unless you act on their recommendations, or have agreed to pay them by the hour.

Some rules of thumb for the DIYers:

- Take research seriously: the best way to educate yourself about different saving and investment plans is to read the personal finance sections of newspapers. If you make a study of the subject, it won't take you long to get the hang of the jargon and basic concepts. Then, before you buy shares, or a financial product such as an insurance policy, read as much about it as you can – whether in a prospectus, annual report, or promotional literature. Make sure you look at the fine print, and really understand what it says, before plunking down your money.

'I never buy a business I don't understand,' says Warren Buffett, the world's most successful investor, who has made billions of dollars for himself and investors in his company, Berkshire Hathaway. To this day, Buffett eschews the latest high-flying bio-tech, Internet, and other high technology stocks, simply because he doesn't know the companies or understand what their products do. Instead, he takes a phlegmatic, plodding approach to investing, with a focus on traditional businesses, such as insurance companies, newspapers and even the largest retail furniture store in his hometown of Omaha, Nebraska. These are recognisable companies with simple, everyday products that everyone uses and can understand.

To paraphrase another of Buffett's great observations: only buy businesses that a fool can run, because chances are someday a fool *will* run them.

- Ask the question, then ask it again: the British have an aversion to asking nosey questions, but when it comes to your money you will have to get over that cultural hang-up. As my friend Charlotte demonstrated, it can be a waste of time and money to accept someone's investment advice without understanding exactly what they are saying (or scribbling).

  It's simple: if you don't understand what someone is

telling you, or what a product is, then ask the question. If you still don't understand, then ask again. Don't let a broker or agent hide behind big words and lofty financial concepts; get them to explain it in plain English. If the person you are questioning can't, or won't, answer in a way that is intelligible, then maybe they don't understand what they are saying themselves. In that case, walk quickly away, and find someone else to talk to.

If you are contemplating an investment, ask yourself: is this the right way for me to spend my money? Will it still be right for me in the future? After all, it doesn't do you any good to lock yourself into a long-term investment if you think you're going to need that money in a year or two.

- Always consider risk. Every investment has risk, but it's a question of degree; you need to decide what sort of risk-reward balance you are comfortable with. If someone tells you an investment is 'risk-free' that's your cue to head out the door – it's never true.

- Shop for the best deal: the market for saving and investment vehicles is highly competitive, and you should use that fact to your advantage. It always pays to comparison shop for the best insurance scheme, unit trust, or ISA. Commission fees, rates of return, and services provided do vary – often significantly.

- Be organised: with new tax rules in effect, you'll need to keep track of every bit of paper generated by your personal money management scheme. Pay special attention to the many documents generated by your investments, dividends and capital gains. Create a file, or files, and be meticulous about keeping your records current.

WHAT TO DO IF THINGS GO WRONG?

There are times when things between a client and a financial professional don't work out. The best way to deal with a disagreement is to talk to the adviser, explain your complaint and give them a chance to set things right. If you remain unhappy, the adviser should tell you how to proceed from there. If you continue to have problems, contact the Financial Services Authority (FSA) on 0845 606 1234. If you can prove you lost money due to the way your investment was handled, it's possible that you are entitled to compensation from the adviser. If the firm you were working with collapses, and you lose money, you may also be able to claim compensation (although there are limites to the amount you will be paid).

Unfortunately, the most common approach to money management is the ostrich strategy, when people stick their heads in the sand and hope against logic that all of their financial worries will magically resolve themselves. If you follow this approach, you are only guaranteeing yourself a big headache.

Presumably, you are reading this book to learn healthy new financial habits – which sometimes means turning to others for advice. This can be intimidating. Indeed, I know from personal experience how hard it is to get motivated, change old routines and take positive action. But what is the alternative? When you think about it in Zen terms, *not* taking action is in itself a form of action – a self-defeating action, that is. Ignoring your high-interest debt while using your credit card to buy non-essentials isn't going to help you buy the house of your dreams; similarly, not investing in proper insurance and not contributing to your employer's pension scheme can have ruinous results for you and your entire family.

Yet, you shouldn't feel compelled to take the entire burden on your own shoulders. It can be equally dangerous, or naïve, to think you can do it all yourself all of the time. There is no shame in getting more information or advice – after all, you can always say no. Sometimes turning to expert help can give you a realistic appraisal of where your finances stand now, and lay out a better course for the future.

It is important to note, however, that this is not a licence to abdicate your own responsibility. Ultimately, *you* are in charge of your money; whether you use professional advice or not, *you* have the greatest say on what happens to it. Getting a planner is not like getting a seeing-eye dog or a financial psychic, after all. Hiring a planner, or devising your own plan, is simply one means to a larger end: building your money for your life.

Turn and Run If:

1) You are told you must buy now or the offer or deal will disappear.
2) Someone suggests you put money into a special deal which they can't explain in detail and which doesn't have any proper documents.
3) Someone suggests you put all your money in one investment.
4) The adviser keeps suggesting you sell your current investments and buy new ones. Done to excess, this is called 'churning'. Advisers do well out of it because they get commission or fees for every deal, but you could lose out unless the investments rise in value by more than your costs.

(*Source*: Financial Services Authority)

CHAPTER 10

PUTTING THE LESSONS TOGETHER: A COMMON-SENSE GUIDE TO GROWING YOUR MONEY FOR YOUR LIFE

I was raised on a farm in the American South, and while this may sound like a romantic childhood to some people, it was not. My family and I had to work hard just to survive. But the experience did teach me some valuable lessons in economy. While I can hardly claim to have green fingers today – one friend says the only species of flora that could survive around me is a dried hydrangea – I do think of managing money wisely as akin to planting and tending a (financial) garden. At first, out of necessity, I had to learn how to grow my own money. After making a few mistakes, I became increasingly interested in the market, and financially self-confident; lately, I have used my experience toiling on Wall Street to help others understand their money and how to grow it.

To make a successful garden, you don't simply throw a handful of mixed seeds on to a random plot and walk away. Similarly, it's not much of a financial plan to throw your money at random investments and hope to strike it rich. Careful gardeners plot their garden out beforehand, with an idea of how it will look once it flowers; they work out which seeds to plant, where the sunlight is, and build in enough time to weed, fertilise and irrigate. Similarly, careful investors meticulously plot where every penny of their money will go, and build into their plans the flexibility to adapt to changing conditions.

As I mentioned at the beginning of this book, I hope you learn from my experience and mistakes. Here, at the end of the book, I'd like to leave you with a few of the key lessons I've learned that don't fit snugly into the preceding chapters – including ways to use your own idiosyncratic habits and personality traits to your advantage.

ASK YOURSELF: WHAT DO I REALLY WANT TO ACHIEVE?

Most of us don't set concrete goals and stick to them; more often, we drift from day to day, focusing on the things in front of our noses that have to be done *right now*. In this way, our time is eaten up by the mundane, necessary details of everyday exis-tence. In this mode, we tend to see the world step by step, rather than pulling back to see the whole path. But when it comes to planning your financial goals, it is essential that you take a long-term view, and have at least a vague idea of where it is you want to go (even if you change your mind about your ultimate destination en route).

It is not, for example, a useful investment goal to simply say 'I want to be rich'. It is much more helpful to set specific goals, such as: 'I want to own a house that I can live in comfortably.' Or, 'As I get older I want to scale down my daily expenses and use the money I save to travel.' Or, 'In my early years I'd like to invest in stocks that will rise in price, but in my later years I want to buy securities that generate a steady income.' These are all very attainable goals, and the hardest part is choosing which one to focus on.

If you're struggling with this, take a practical tip: write down a list of possible life-scenarios and what you'd like to achieve financially, and then prioritise them. Be as realistic as you can. This exercise may appear simplistic, but somehow the physical act of writing can jog the mind in unexpected ways, and seeing your ideas on the page tends to make them real – especially if you revisit your list a few days later.

PUT A PRICE TAG ON YOUR DREAMS

The next step is to translate your various life-scenarios into real numbers and consider how much money it's going to take to achieve your goals. This exercise is, at heart, a reality-check – and it has proven an important tool for me and my clients.

I sometimes recommend that my American students go to one of the financial web sites on the Internet and work through a retirement-planning checklist: these sites ask you to itemise your dreams, and then put an estimated value on them (including projected rates of inflation). The result? Nearly everyone is dumbfounded by the cost of their future.

You can do the same thing with a pen and a piece of paper: write down your specific goals, and then put a value to them (rounding up to the higher number) – the cost of renovating your kitchen, say, or travelling to Tibet, buying a new suit or a used motorbike, eating at three star Parisian restaurants, or even the cost of building a simple garden in the back yard. Most people find the future to be a lot more expensive than they had originally imagined.

This exercise strikes some as crass, or unnecessary: why should everything have a price tag attached to it? they wonder. Well, the answer is simple: almost everything in life – other than breathing – *does* come at a cost, and you might as well be realistic about the price of your dreams. The realism hopefully promotes action.

If you ignore life's future price tags now, you'll still have to confront them at some point – and they almost always grow bigger with time. Think of it in terms of shopping: everyone has seen something in a shop window that catches their fancy; they hesitate to buy it, and when they return the price is inevitably higher (or the item is gone). I have witnessed this scenario over and over again when people think about preparing themselves for the future. They say they *want* to do the right thing, but they don't turn their thoughts into action; later, when they *have* to buy insurance, write a will, or set up a pension, they inevitably find that the cost of doing these things has risen. The bottom line is that everything costs something – whether in real money or in lost opportunity.

The future is expensive, but don't let the numbers deter you. As with gardening, your financial plans should be flexible, and you should be willing to alter your ideas as you go along. Let's say you go shopping for a tree for your garden, and you discover that the rare Japanese Maple you had dreamed of is outrageously expensive; at this juncture, you must be realistic and tell yourself that while you can still plant a tree in the garden it's going to have to be another *kind* of tree. This is not all that different from deciding to take a less expensive holiday or invest in a less risky security.

UNDERSTAND RISK

Risk is simply a fact of trying to grow your money, as it is in trying to grow seeds into sustainable crops. You should be *aware* of risk, but not *scared* of it.

Some seeds germinate, and some don't. It's not always your fault when a financial decision doesn't work out as planned. As in farming, you can't always control the forces affecting you – the market may be down, or real estate prices may suddenly sky-rocket – but you can't let these circumstances deter you, either. The best defence is a solid plan, flexibility and fortitude.

LEARN TO USE YOUR STRENGTHS AND WEAKNESSES

We all have inherent strengths and weaknesses, and sometimes personality traits that we have long perceived as weaknesses can prove to be strengths when used in a new context. Indeed, it is in facing our weaknesses head-on that we often make the greatest strides in self-improvement.

My grandmother once said of me: 'You're never satisfied.' At the time, I considered this a damning observation, and for years worried that I suffered a great weakness of character. But when I went to Wall Street, I learned that this trait – what I now think of as a 'restlessness' or 'curiosity' rather than dissatisfaction – was a great boon. The stock market is ever-changing and unpredictable, and to keep up with it you need to be able to adapt to rapid shifts and be open to new ideas. Much to my surprise, I found that I was naturally comfortable in this environment. With time, my love of the new led me to specialise in technology stocks, which is a dynamic investment area. Indeed, the longer I spent in the market the more interested I became – not in hoarding money, but in the way money works and people interact with it.

Indeed, the serendipitous nature of the market reminds me of the chance encounters you can sometimes have walking the streets of New York or London – the quick meetings that can linger in your mind for years, or change your life. This kind of place, I discovered, is the natural habitat for my restless, change-loving personality.

Now, I encourage people to transfer their own traits, habits, or skills from one realm of life to another – and especially to the financial arena. Take the case of my young friends Carl and Polly, who wanted to buy a car. To them, a car represented 'freedom', 'mobility' and a certain lifestyle they aspired to. They are not careful with their money in general, but Carl and Polly wanted a car so badly they were able to save up and buy one. What they didn't realise is that the adjectives they used to describe their car can be applied to other aspects of their lives – the freedom to change jobs, the mobility to travel for work or on holiday, the lifestyle afforded by a new home. As with a car, they have to make sacrifices and save up for these things. When I mentioned this,

Carl and Polly groaned. But when I pointed out that they had already learned the saving habit and could transfer the discipline they had employed to buy a car to their new goals, they smiled.

Do you recognise yourself anywhere in the following list of personality traits?

Acquisitive

I will admit to a certain Warhol-like tendency to collect objects that I find beautiful. At one time, I owned a collection of sixty-nine antique chairs, but when I figured out how much money I had locked up in chairs, and what my collection was costing me for insurance and storage, I began to de-accession. Nonetheless, the hoarding instinct remained intact. Rather than buy more chairs, I channelled my energy and money into securities. Soon, I found great satisfaction in picking unheralded stocks and watching the numbers in my bank account – rather than the number of chairs I had stored away – grow. Every additional zero to my total became a reason to celebrate, and proved as thrilling as unearthing a piece of vintage Wedgwood in the back of a dusty shop.

Risk-taking

My friend Gillian is a born gambler. She likes to go bungee-jumping for fun, and complained that there was 'no fizz' in investing in safe, long-term securities. However, when she tried speculating on the derivatives market – a very risky (and potentially lucrative) form of investment – she found her niche. She is obviously happiest when on the edge.

Risk-averse

Doug, on the other hand, is a very steady personality who enjoys fishing and helping others. His ambition has always been to keep his life simple, and he is happy to admit, 'I'm not driven. I like to take it easy.' Doug worked in a bank: he decided to save up a few hundred thousand dollars – not a fortune – and once he reached his savings goal, he retired at age forty-six. Now he devotes himself to charity work . . . and the pursuit of smallmouth bass.

Organised

When people meet me today, they see a man whose kitchen is hospital-ward clean, whose chest of drawers is full of perfectly arranged socks and pressed underwear, and whose closet is hung with shirts that are starched, pressed and arranged by colour (a frightening picture, isn't it?). Naturally, they assume that I have always been this way about every aspect of my life – especially my personal finances. But as you know from reading this book, that is not quite the truth.

I was raised in a cluttered house, lived a quasi-bohemian existence for a time (my Blue Period), and was probably more budget-challenged and credit-card addicted than most people. The handwriting was on the wall for me, however, and when my nose was pressed firmly *into* the wall – by a series of financial setbacks – I learned that I had to get organised to stave off the impending chaos. I faced my weakness and changed my ways, and am better off for it. Now I've gone off to the opposite extreme, and have become hyper-organised. It's not for everybody, but it works for me.

Generous

Some people are driven to help others, and sacrifice themselves, to a fault. If you are a person whose first instinct is to give any extra money you have to family or friends, you should think twice. To do a really good turn for the family, you should be sure that your *own* needs are met first. If you reach retirement age without taking proper precautions for your care, for example, you will become a burden. The anxiety your family and friends will feel over you will outweigh the nice things you've done for them in the past. The lesson: be as generous to yourself as you are to others.

Instinctual

It was in central London, in 1989, when I first used a cashpoint machine to withdraw a ten-pound note from my bank account in America. I was absolutely gob-smacked: the brilliant simplicity of the transaction spoke to me immediately. I felt that I intuitively understood the company and its product, and could see how the electronic transfer of information around the world could be applied to many endeavours (I was hardly alone in this realisation, of course). I asked all of my technology-mad friends about it, and researched the company behind the cashpoints. Satisfied that my instincts had been right, I bought the company's stock and held on to it; today, a decade later, the company has spread around the world and is the industry leader. It pays to trust your gut-feelings when looking for new investments.

Social

If you're a 'joiner', the type of person who enjoys group activities – you prefer to go to a gym for exercise, say, or you join Weight Watchers in order to diet – then you might consider joining an investment club. Every month, thousands of people of every stripe use these clubs to learn how to invest, save money, make friends and educate themselves.

ProShare, the investment club advisory body (0207 394 5200), suggests the following tips for starting an investment club:

- Gather a few friends – you only need one or two at first – who might be interested in an investment club.
- Hold an exploratory meeting: discuss the idea of a club; explain that members will be expected to contribute financially and attend meetings regularly; make sure that everyone's opinions and research into shares are taken into account. At the end of the meeting, ask participants to reconfirm their interest in an investment club.
- Hold an inaugural meeting. At this meeting you need to:

- Elect the club's chairman, secretary and treasurer
- Choose a name for the club
- Decide how much you are going to invest each month
- Pick a meeting place (an office, your home, a pub), and establish a regular meeting time
- Adopt the rules and constitution for your club
- Open a bank account into which subscriptions will be paid (a treasurer's or clubs and societies account at most high street banks is usually the best)
- Discuss investment policy, even though you may want to wait until you have sufficient money in the club fund before you make your first investment
- Appoint a stockbrocker

After careful research, your club will then be ready to invest in its first share.

Anti-social (or simply *Pressed for Time*)

If, on the other hand, you dislike groups, or simply don't have the time for a regularly scheduled club meeting, then perhaps you should consider going on-line, and investigate some of the personal finance sites, research potential investments, get new ideas, or sign up for a web-based brokerage account and start trading electronically. You can do this at the crack of dawn, in the middle of the night, or from your desk during the day.

Compartmentalising

It used to be that every April and August my credit card bills would quadruple. These are the months when the New York clothing stores hold their big sales – unlike the Christmas sales, these spring and fall sales are quieter, and known for being ripe with 'real value'. The problem was, I was so seduced by the value that I invariably overspent. I compartmentalised this glaring fact in my mind by telling myself I was finding great 'bargains'.

There *was* a lot of individual value there, of course, but in the aggregate I was spending more than ever.

After much soul-searching, I was able to turn my habit of compartmentalising into a useful savings tool. I still go to the sales, but now my rule is I can buy anything I want, as long as it is only *one* item. I put the money I would have formerly spent on too many bargains into my retirement account. It's a psychological trick I play on myself: once I write a cheque, I feel that the money is gone, and I cease to think about it; it's as if I had spent the money on clothes – only a retirement fund is much more valuable and long lasting.

Maybe one or more of these personality traits describes you; maybe there's another characteristic that fits you better. No matter; there's a successful financial style that will work for you, whatever you're like. The challenge is, first, to know yourself; then, to apply what you know to handling your money intelligently.

The difference between someone who doesn't understand how money works, and someone who does is like the difference between a dirt farmer who slaves in his field just to survive and an ornamental gardener who tends her topiary or tomatoes with a spirit of creativity, joy and inner peace. Ideally, your financial garden should be a respite for you, a meaningful hobby that both sustains and satisfies you. That is not to say it is easy.

In both gardening and finance, change and risk are constant: outside forces (nature and the markets) will behave unpredictably; loss is always possible, yet patience and diligence are ultimately rewarded. The choice of what you plant and where you plant it is important. And some experimentation is necessary – after all, what seems logical on paper may not necessarily bear fruit in the real world. Yet, with a little work, and luck, there's a good possibility that your money will grow and grow – and produce real money for your life.

INDEX